OUT-OF-THE-BODY EXPERIENCES
A FOURTH ANALYSIS

OTHER WORKS BY DR. ROBERT CROOKALL:

Coal Measure Plants, Edward Arnold & Co., Ltd., 1929
The Kidston Collection of Fossil Plants, H.M. Stationery Office, 1938
Fossil Plants of the Carboniferous Rocks of Great Britain, H.M. Stationery Office, Part I, 1955; Part II, 1959; Part III, 1964; Part IV, 1966
The Study and Practice of Astral Projection, Aquarian Press, 1960; American Edition, University Books, Inc., New Hyde Park, New York, 1966
More Astral Projection, Aquarian Press, 1964
The Techniques of Astral Projection, Aquarian Press, 1964
The Supreme Adventure, James Clarke & Co., Ltd., 1961
Intimations of Immortality, James Clarke & Co., Ltd., 1965
During Sleep: The Possibility of "Co-operation," Theosophical Publishing House, London, 1964
The Next World—and the Next: Ghostly Garments, Theosophical Publishing House, London, 1966
Events on the Threshold of the After-Life, Darshana International, Moradabad, India, 1967
The Mechanisms of Astral Projection, Darshana International, Moradabad, India, 1968

Scientific Papers in:

The Geological Magazine / *The Annals of Botany* / *The Memoirs of the Geological Survey of Great Britain* / *The Naturalist* / *Memoirs and Proceedings of the Manchester Literary and Philosophic Society* / *Proceedings of the Geologists' Association* / *Proceedings of the Royal Society of Edinburgh* / *Proceedings of the Royal Physical Society* / *Proceedings of the Cotteswold Naturalist and Field Club* / *Proceedings of the Institute of Mining Engineers* / *Proceedings of the South Wales Institute of Engineers* / *Fuel* / *Colliery Guardian* / *Darshana International* / *Psychics International* / *World Science Review* / *The British Association for the Advancement of Science*

Books in Preparation:

Ecstasy and Its Significance
"Dreams" of High Significance
Experiences on the Threshold of the After-Life
Life—"a Cheat" or "a Sacred Burden"?
Greater than We Know
The Hereafter

With Dr. F. B. A. Welch:

British Regional Geology: Bristol and Gloucester District, H.M. Stationery Office, 1935

OUT-OF-THE-BODY EXPERIENCES / A FOURTH ANALYSIS

BY

ROBERT CROOKALL

B.Sc. (Psychology), D.Sc., Ph.D.

Late Principal Geologist, H.M. Geological Survey (Department of Scientific and Industrial Research), London / Formerly Lecturer in Botany, University of Aberdeen / Member of the Society for Psychical Research / Hon. Life Member of the Indian Society for Psychical and Yogic Research / Member of the Churches' Fellowship for Psychical and Spiritual Studies / Hon. Member of the American Society for Psychical Research

THE CITADEL PRESS / SECAUCUS, N.J.

Second paperbound printing

Copyright © 1970 by Robert Crookall
All rights reserved
Published by Citadel Press
A division of Lyle Stuart Inc.
120 Enterprise Ave., Secaucus, N.J. 07094
In Canada: George J. McLeod Limited, Toronto
Manufacture in the United States of America
ISBN 0–8065–0610–5

CONTENTS

7

THIRD PART

Discussion

Contents

9

PREFACE

When, as has often fallen to the lot of the present writer, one undertakes the microscopic investigation of a petrified stem, it is necessary to take transparent slices, "sections," of it from various angles. The first series of sections is made across the stem, the second series goes down its middle, and the third is tangential. This procedure leaves no tissue unrevealed.

The investigation of out-of-the-body experiences demands an analogous psychological procedure: that is, one analyzes the testimonies of those who claim to have had them, from various angles. When completed, this also leaves nothing unrevealed. Our work to date is published in some half-dozen books.*

Our detailed analyses of the testimonies at once revealed a highly significant pattern of events that had occurred and of experiences that had been undergone—a pattern that those who previously investigated the subject had overlooked. A replica-body, or "double," was "born" from the physical body and took up a position above it.

* Crookall, R., *The Study and Practice of Astral Projection,* Aquarian Press, 1961 (out of print); American edition, 1967, by University Books, Inc., New Hyde Park, N.Y.; *More Astral Projections,* Aquarian Press, 1964; *The Techniques of Astral Projection, ibid.; Events on the Threshold of the After-life,* Darshana International, Moradabad, India, 1967; *Experiences on the Threshold of the After-life, ibid.; The Mechanisms of Astral Projection, ibid.*

As the "double" separated from the body, there was a "blackout" in consciousness (much as the changing of gears in a car causes a momentary break in the transmission of power). There was often a panoramic review of the past life, and the vacated physical body was commonly seen from the released "double." Then came a noteworthy observation: The "double" was not, in fact, completely detached from the body. On the contrary, the two remained united by an extension of their substance which clearly corresponds to the "silver cord" of the Scriptures. Peter Urquhart (our Case No. 170), for example, having merely relaxed, left his body: He stated, "After the first experience I realized what was meant in Ecclesiastes by 'the silver cord.' . . . I had read that famous verse (xii,6) and it had remained in my mind, but until the experience I had not the slightest idea what it meant; it just seemed a poetic image. Certainly I had no idea that it referred to a link between body and Soul, and I had no idea of this separation until I actually experienced it myself."

An American medical man, Dr. R. B. Hout (our Case No. 153), observed the "cord" that "united the spirit body with the physical" in the case of other people, namely, three patients whose "doubles" had been forcibly ejected by anesthetics. This doctor also observed the "cord" that formed, for a time, when his aunt was in the process of dying, that is, when her "double" was leaving her body permanently. He stated, "I had not read of the actual process of the Soul leaving the body, and I had not known of the 'cord' that connects the spirit-body with the earth-body." Yet he described his aunt's "silver cord" as "a translucent luminous silver radiance" that was about an inch in diameter. He said, "The 'cord' seemed alive with vibrant energy. I could see the pulsations of 'light' stream along the course of it. . . . With each pulsation the spirit-body became more alive and denser, whereas the physical body became more nearly lifeless." At length, "the last connecting-strand of the 'silver cord' snapped and the spirit-body was free."

An eminent American clergyman, Dr. R. J. Staver, similarly saw the release of his father's "spirit-body" or "double" as he was dying—with a feature which "reminded" him of the "silver cord" of Ecclesiastes. Such similar accounts by trustworthy people cannot be dismissed as mere imagination and, if admitted, the "doubles" cannot have been mental images, since mental images in general are not equipped with extensions.

To continue with the pattern of events revealed in testimonies concerning temporary out-of-the-body experiences. Contrary to what one would expect, no one described pain or fear as having been caused by leaving the body—everything seemed perfectly natural. The persons concerned, moreover, commonly realized that the "double" was the primary body for thought and feeling, while the physical body (with which we all normally, and not unnaturally, tend to identify ourselves) was merely a secondary, and a temporary, instrument via which earth-life is rendered possible. Consciousness, as it operated through the separated "double," was more extensive than in ordinary life (when it operates first through the "double" and then through the physical body with its sense organs): There were sometimes telepathy, clairvoyance, and foreknowledge. "Dead" friends were often seen. Many of the deponents expressed great reluctance to re-enter the body and so return to earth-life (whereas, of course, most people regard leaving the body at death as the greatest of evils). As the "double" did reassociate with the body, there was a "blackout" in consciousness similar to that which had occurred at the beginning of the experience, when they dissociated. We summarize our conclusion up to this point as follows:

This general pattern of events in out-of-the-body experiences, hitherto unrecognized, cannot be explained adequately on the hypothesis that all such experiences were dreams and that all the "doubles" described were mere mental images (of physical bodies), i.e., hallucinations. It can, on the other hand, be readily explained on the hypothesis that these were genuine experiences and that the "doubles" seen were objective (though ultraphysical) bodies.

Our second type of analysis of the testimonies consisted of a contrast between the two very distinct conditions under which out-of-the-body experiences occur, i.e., naturally (and therefore gradually), on the one hand, and forcibly (and therefore suddenly), on the other. The last-mentioned cases include those induced by falls and the administration of anesthetics.

Two patterns, subsidiary to the general pattern mentioned above, emerged. People who quitted their bodies in a natural manner enjoyed consciousness of a clear, extensive, and often supernormal type—that is, with telepathy, and so on; while the consciousness of the forcibly ejected was remarkably restricted, dim, and even subnormal—that is, with dreamlike elements. Those who left naturally tended to glimpse bright and peaceful ("Paradise") conditions, a kind of glorious earth; while the forcibly ejected, if not on earth, tended to be in the relatively dim, confused, and semi-dreamlike conditions that correspond to the "Hades" of the ancients. The former met many helpers (including the "dead" friends and relatives already mentioned); the latter sometimes encountered discarnate would-be hinderers.

This subsidiary pattern of events and experiences, like the general pattern, cannot be explained on the assumption that all was imagined. On the other hand, it is adequately explained on the hypothesis that the experiences were genuine and that the "doubles" were objective (though ultra-physical) bodies that could include (a) a "semi-physical" feature which we call the vehicle of vitality and (b) a "super-physical" Soul Body. These had presumably been drawn from, and would eventually be returned to, corresponding portions of the total earth—those which are called "Hades" and "Paradise" respectively—see the writer's *The Next World—and the Next* (Theosophical Publishing House, 1966, p. 63). There is, as the ancients declared, a close correspondence between man, the microcosm, and the Universe, the macrocosm.

A third type of analysis involved a contrast between the testimonies provided by two different kinds of people who had out-of-the-body experiences: On the one hand, ordinary folk; and, on the other, the relatively rare people whose vehicles of vitality are loosely associated with their physical bodies—those of the mediumistic bodily constitution (whether aware of it or not). It was found that the latter commonly made an observation that was never made by ordinary folk (which observation has hitherto passed unnoticed): It was that something that resembled "mist," "fog," "smoke," "vapor," or "cloud" left their bodies and formed part of the liberated "double." The "mist" was identified as substance from the vehicle of vitality (something that corresponds to the ectoplasm of psychical research). This difference also points to genuine out-of-the-body experiences that involve objective (ultra-physical) bodies, and not to imagined experiences and imaginary bodies.

In *Events on the Threshold of the After-Life,* we mentioned a number of cases in which percipients saw "doubles" that formed in two stages: On p. 57 Mrs. "V" was cited as having first seen a "light"; this turned into a "cloud" and, in the "cloud," her sister's face appeared. It transpired that her sister had just died. Mrs. "V" was not out of her body; but "Kenwood," cited on p. 27, when out of his body, saw first something like a star and then his "dead" father's "double." Fitzsimmons (p. 61) first saw a "luminous cloud"; then his "dead" mother appeared in it. Tweedale (p. 58) reported the two-stage formation of materialized figures: There was first a "luminous cloud" and this turned into a definite figure.

These were firsthand observations. "Communicators" (necessarily via mediums) made similar statements. On p. 109 we cited Keeler's "communicator" as saying the spirits "take on the emanation of earth" and then can appear in definite human form. On p. 110 the "communicators" of Leaf, Stead, Smith, and Taylor and Bedford were cited as making similar statements. These "communications" correspond to the above firsthand observations.

The dissolution of materialized figures, according to Tweedale (p. 58), also takes place in two stages (as might be expected)—the "apparently solid" materialized figure becomes "a luminous cloud" and then disappears.

In the present study we take still another "section"

through the testimonies: We show that, while some "doubles" leave (and reenter) the body in a single stage, others do so in two distinct stages. It is scarcely necessary to say that no mental images appear (and disappear) in two distinct stages.

Readers who have had experiences such as these may send details to the writer at 9, Lansdown Road Mansions, Bath, BA1, 5ST, England.

ROBERT CROOKALL

INTRODUCTION

"Astral projection is 'the most significant' of all psychical phenomena."—*F. W. H. Myers*

"If astral projection is a true and natural phenomenon, then all psychic manifestations must be reviewed from a new light."—*J.A.S.P.R., 1937*

"The exploration of outer space is far more exciting than the conquest of the poles . . . , yet it only promises to give us more knowledge of the physical cosmos, valuable as that will be."—*Sir Alister Hardy, F.R.S.*

"Space flights are merely an escape, a fleeing-away from oneself, because it is easier to go to Mars than it is to penetrate one's own being—it symbolises a state of complete anxiety in man."—*Miguel Serrano*

"The soul of man is so vast that you will never find its boundaries by travelling in any direction."—*Heracleitus* (576–480 B.C.)

"The spirit world was never an invention in the sense that fire-boring was an invention; it was far rather an experience, the conscious acceptance of a reality in no way inferior to that of the material world."—*C. G. Jung*

"I knew a Christian man who (whether in the body or out of it, I do not know—God knows) was caught up as far as the third heaven. And I know that the same man . . . was caught up into Paradise, and heard words so secret that human lips may not repeat them."—*St. Paul* (II Cor. xii, 2–5)

"Many questions, many mysteries remain. And possibly the most important and most fundamental of them all is, whether the inner adventures of the occultists are always merely fantasy, or whether, sometimes at least, they are experiences that do relate to an external reality."—*Douglas Hall* and *Pat Williams*

"True science will not deny the existence of things because they cannot be weighed or measured. It will rather lead us to believe that the wonders and subtleties of possible existence surpass all that our mental powers allow us to perceive. . . . We must ignore no existence whatever. . . . If a phenomenon does *exist*, it demands some kind of *explanation*."—*William Stanley Jevons*

From the dawn of history to the present time, people have claimed to have left their bodies in various circumstances, to have retained consciousness, and subsequently to have reentered their bodies: Many said that they possessed a second body, one which was a replica, or "double," of the physical. Such a case is mentioned in the Scriptures.[1] St. Paul[2] insisted: "There is such a thing as an animal body; there is also a 'spiritual' body." That which he called the "spiritual" body others called the "astral" (bright) or "etheric" (tenuous) body. We call it the Soul Body.

As already said, many people have made this remarkable claim. Some skeptics, however, have tried to make out that they merely copied each other's accounts. That suggestion is inadmissable, however, since a number of descriptions have been given by quite young children (twenty-two cases of the kind being included in the present writer's *More Astral Projections*[3] and many others in his *Astral Projection and Survival*). Again, illiterate adults have provided numerous typical cases; for example, Dr. B. J. F. Laubscher,[4] the eminent psychiatrist of Port Elizabeth, Republic of South Africa, published a number from natives who could not read and who spoke only Africaans—their narratives had to be translated into English. Primitives also have the experience of leaving the body, as is shown by Professor M. Eliade.[5] Thus we have testimonies concerning these important matters—apart from "Westerners"—from ancient Chinese and Tibetans, Indian Yogis, Red Indians, Gold Coast natives, Basutos, natives of Eastern Siberia, Mongolia, and Oceania (and from an Icelander who could speak only his own language).

Dr. Audrey Butt (*Trances,* 1967, p. 93) wrote of the Amazonian Indians: "The human spirit ["double"] in some cases has the ability to detach itself from the body of its own volition in order to achieve certain ends." She continued, "The shaman is master of this technique during trance, but others also, who are not shamans, are believed to be able to project their 'spirits': this is done by will-power or sometimes with the aid of special charms. . . ."

Apart from this evidence as to the general reliability of the testimonies, there are numerous descriptions that have been given by persons of high professional standing —doctors, clergymen, professors, and scientists—whose word cannot reasonably be doubted by any unbiased person. Professor Hornell Hart (*International Journal of Parapsychology,* 1967, p. 49) observed, "Reports of pro-

jections have had world-wide distribution over centuries"; and Professor Charles T. Tart (*ibid.*, p. 251)
said, "Because of its apparently universal distribution
across cultures and throughout history, out-of-the-body
experience constitutes what Jung termed an archetypal
experience—an experience potentially available to many
members of the human race simply by virtue of being
human."

We discussed the possibility of copied, invented, or
exaggerated accounts, in *The Techniques of Astral Projection* (1964, p. xx) and *Intimations of Immortality*
(1965, p. 14).

There can be no reasonable doubt that genuine out-of-
the-body experiences occur. The explanation of an experience (awareness of being out of the body) or of a
phenomenon (the possession of a duplicate, ultra-physical body)—that is, the hypothesis by which the testimonies can be most satisfactorily explained—is another
matter. Certain medical men hold the hypothesis that
illness, especially hysteria, causes the phenomenon (sug-
gesting that the accounts are suspect). Other medicos
adopt the hypothesis that all "doubles" are imaginary:
that, since we all form a mental image of our own bodies,
when unwell, we may suppose that we see that image.
Among those who hold this latter hypothesis is the
eminent psychiatrist Dr. Stafford-Clark, M.D., F.R.C.P.,
D.P.M., physician in charge of the Department of Psychological Medicine, Guy's Hospital. He expounded that
view on television not long ago. A still more eminent
psychiatrist, Dr. C. G. Jung, also held that the "double"
is always subjective in nature but, instead of regarding it

as an imagined mental image, he considered it to be an "archetype" in the Collective Unconscious.

"Who," asked Alexander Pope, "shall decide when doctors disagree?" The answer demands the elucidation of a prior question, namely, "What were the *facts* concerning which the doctors' *hypotheses* differed?" Actually, not one of these doctors first assembled all the available facts ("stubborn things"!) and then, having stated their hypotheses, applied them in detail to all the facts, showing how admirably they explained them all— not just a few selected ones. Benjamin Whichcote, Provost of King's, said, "He that gives reason for what he saith has done what is fit to be done and the most that can be done. He that gives no reason speaks nothing, though he saith never so much."

In *More Astral Projections*[6] we cited numerous facts that are readily explicable on our hypothesis that many of the "doubles" that have been described by people who had out-of-the-body experiences were not subjective— were neither mere mental images nor "archetypes" in the "unconscious"—but were objective (though ultra-physical, not, of course, physical). Dr. Stafford-Clark and Dr. C. G. Jung were not aware of the existence of these facts, and therefore did not endeavor to account for them on the basis of their hypotheses. We said, "While it cannot be doubted that we do all form mental images of our bodies, and that sick folk occasionally suppose that they see their own mental images, the other, the 'astral body' hypothesis, best explains numerous facts. Thus it is not, as some doctors suppose, a case of *either* the objective *or* the subjective explanation: we maintain that they are wrong in claiming that *all* 'doubles' are imaginary—on the contrary, we hold that the facts indicate that many, very many, are objective. Those who say that all are subjective have 'emptied out the baby with the bath-water.' Moreover, the subjective, imaginary cases are of personal interest only; the objective cases are of the utmost importance to the whole of humanity."

We owe the first definite step toward the solution of this important problem to a young American, Sylvan J. Muldoon, of Darlington, Wisconsin. In 1929, in collaboration with Dr. Hereward Carrington, the eminent psychical researcher, he published *The Projection of the Astral Body*.[7] In this he gave descriptions, based on his own experiences beginning when he was a boy of twelve years, of hundreds of astral projections. Muldoon invited his readers to apply certain methods so they could prove for themselves the reality of the experience. He promised, "You will no longer doubt that the individual can exist apart from his physical body. No longer will you be forced to accept theories . . . for you will have proof for yourself—as sure and as self-evident as the fact that you are physically alive." In 1936 Muldoon published *The Case for Astral Projection*,[8] containing numerous case histories of others. Further case histories were given by Muldoon and Carrington in *The Phenomena of Astral Projection*.[9]

It should be noted that the present writer, while agreeing (on the basis of the available facts) that astral projections are genuine experiences, does not recommend indiscriminate attempts to project. Projections may become unbidden, when one is "ready." If forced, there may be highly undesirable results. No one who is not mentally and emotionally stable and controlled should try to obtain any psychical experience, for "fools rush in where angels fear to tread."

It is the implications of the phenomena that are important. More than a century ago, Catherine Crowe[10] wrote, "By annihilating the necessities of the body we may loosen the bonds of the Spirit [which uses the objective "doubles"] and enable it to manifest some of its inherent endowments. Ascetics and saints have frequently done this voluntarily, and disease or a peculiar [the mediumistic] constitution sometimes do it for us involuntarily. *While it is undesirable that we should seek to produce such a state, it is extremely desirable that we should avail ourselves of the instruction to be gained by the knowledge that such phenomena exist and that thereby our connexion with the spiritual world may become a demonstrable fact.*" These are wise words.

In 1956 Professor Hornell Hart, Director of the International Project for Research on ESP Projection, in *Proceedings of the Society for Psychical Research*,[11] published significant studies which very strongly suggested that astral projections are genuine experiences and that the "astral body" is objective. He compared the phantasms ("doubles") of the living, as described by astral projectors and others, with those of the dead. He pointed out that in the former the projector was conscious that he had left his body and that he was in a different scene. This, Professor Hart suggested, may also apply to "doubles" of the dead. If "doubles" of the living can be used as instruments of consciousness, then the same may well apply to the "doubles" of the dead—survival is strongly suggested on those grounds alone. (The present writer has also made a comparison among the "doubles" of the living, of the dying, and of the dead, though from an angle different from that of Professor Hornell Hart. The study is entitled *The Mechanisms of Astral Projection*.)[12]

In *The Supreme Adventure*,[13] we classified and analyzed numerous psychic "communications" which purported to describe what had occurred at the permanent release from the body, which, to us, is death. Our method consisted in instituting a contrast between what was described (a) in cases of natural, and therefore gradual, death and (b) in cases of enforced, and therefore sudden, death. A basic pattern of events and experiences was recognized, as well as certain characteristic differences between natural and enforced transitions. The events included the release, from the physical body, of a duplicate ultra-physical body, the "double"; this at first lay above the body, often horizontally and only a few feet above, often remaining for a short time attached to it by a "silver cord"-extension; the extension snapped and the now completely released "double" uprighted.

The experiences described by the supposed dead often began with a rapid, nonemotional, nonresponsible review of the past life. There was then a "blackout" in consciousness (as the "double" separated from the body) followed by a three-day "sleep," often with dreams (i.e., some awareness of "Hades" conditions); the newly dead man awoke in "Paradise" conditions with expanded consciousness (i.e., with telepathy, clairvoyance, and foreknowledge), and dead friends were seen. Fairly early in the "Paradise" period, a second, more protracted, review of the past life was experienced, one which, unlike the first, was highly emotional and responsible: The newly dead man felt both the joy and the pain that his earth-life words and acts had caused in others, and this experience evidently corresponds to the individual Judgment. Each Soul then gravitated to his appropriate place in the immediate hereafter.

Whereas those who died naturally in old age were tired and tended to sleep (mitigating the shock of transition), those who were killed in the prime of life were active at the time and tended to remain awake; but they were not fully awake and many did not at first realize that they had died. Again, whereas those who "passed" naturally awakened to the bright, clear, and beautiful "Paradise" environment, corresponding to the "super-physical" Soul Body, those whose death was enforced in the prime of life tended to be in the "cloudy," "misty," "foggy," even "watery" "Hades" conditions, corresponding to the "semi-physical" vehicle of vitality. The latter had left the physical body along with the Soul Body and necessarily enshrouded it. Still again, whereas those who "passed" naturally soon underwent their "Judgment" experience, those whose "doubles" were forcibly evicted from their bodies in the prime of life could not pass into "Paradise" and undergo that important experience until after the vehicle of vitality had been shed from the composite "double" (i.e., until the event which is often called the second "death," their "Judgment" was delayed). It may be said that the Reverend Leslie Weatherhead "warmly recommended" *The Supreme Adventure* (in which, as said, we analyzed "communications" received via mediums, as to what occurred at, and soon after, death) as "a splendid summary of serious psychical research findings."

In *The Study and Practice of Astral Projection*[14] and *More Astral Projections*[3] we analyzed 381 testimonies of people who, independently of any medium, claimed to have left their bodies temporarily. The same method was used as with the supposed permanent releases.[13] A similar basic pattern of events and experiences was obtained. A replica body, or "double" (in some cases interpreted as consisting of the "semi-physical" vehicle of vitality only, in others as representing the "super-physical" Soul Body only, and in still others—as at death—as an admixture of the two), rose above the physical body and was often at first horizontal, only a few feet away, and attached to it by a "silver cord"-extension (which did not break).

The experiences also corresponded with what had been said (via mediums) to apply to the permanent releases of "doubles": There was sometimes an early nonemotional review of the past life, a "blackout" in consciousness (as the "double" separated from the body), and an expansion of consciousness, with telepathy, clairvoyance, or foreknowledge, as "Paradise" conditions were glimpsed. Dead friends were often seen. It was also observed that, when the "double" returned to and reentered the body, the events and experiences were the same as in the outward journey, but in reverse order—in some cases the "double" took up a horizontal position a few feet above the body and the reassociation of the two often caused a "blackout" in consciousness.

Not only did the general pattern of events and experiences that were said, via mediums, to occur in permanent release from the body show a significant resemblance to that said, independently of mediums, to occur in temporary releases, but there was a significant agreement, in these two markedly dissimilar circumstances, as to the differences that characterized the natural and enforced releases of the "doubles." The conclusion is inescapable: The "communications" concerning death were not products of the medium concerned; they were genuine and reliable descriptions of their transitions by surviving personalities.

As said, hundreds of people, including quite young children and illiterate adults (obviating copying from the descriptions of others), have claimed that they left their physical bodies. Many of them stated that they were in a second, ultra-physical body which they variously called an "ethereal," "etheric," "astral," "Soul," "psychical," or "spiritual" body. This was a replica, or "double," of the physical body—but it could usually pass through walls and doors without hindrance, was unaffected by gravity, traveled instantly and automatically to any person or place, however distant, whereon the attention was directed. The deponents claimed to have visited (a) other localities on earth (or the "etheric doubles" thereof), (b) localities in the relatively dim "Hades" world (in the denser aura of the earth), and (c) others in the bright and beautiful "Paradise" realms (in the aura of the earth). Some of those who claimed to have visited distant earth localities returned with information which they could not have obtained by the use of the physical senses, later verified by others.

Professor Hornell Hart[15] wrote, "Much in the scientific spirit of F. W. H. Myers, Dr. Crookall has assembled hundreds of cases of two basic types: (1) out-of-the-body experiences and (2) messages through mediums. By a detailed and intensive analysis of the characteristics of these case reports, Dr. Crookall established a *prima facie* case which appears to authenticate the objective reality of the experience thus reported. . . . I have applied a preliminary statistical test to one of his crucial generalisations, and found that it is validated." Again:[16] "The survival hypothesis was explored and sustained in 'The Six Theories about Apparitions' study in 1956. And since that date, R. Crookall and S. Smith have published over four hundred systematically-analysed cases which seem to the author [Hart] to clinch the case."

If, as the present writer maintains, and Professor Hornell Hart agreed, the experiences described by people who left their bodies temporarily, popularly called astral projectors, and those described by deceased persons in relation to their permanent release from the body, are authentic, the question naturally arises, "What is the nature of the 'double,' the nonphysical replica of the physical body, that is so often described?" As already said, some psychiatrists, for example, Professor J. Lehrmitte and Dr. Stafford-Clark, hold the hypothesis that it is imaginary, that it is a mental image of one's own physical body, while others, for example, Dr. C. G. Jung and Dr. Jaffé,[17] say that it is an "archetype" in the "Collective Unconscious." As already said, our hypothesis is that many "doubles" are objective, and that these consist of (a) part of the "semi-physical" vehicle of vitality (the "vital body" of the Rosicrucians, the "etheric double" of the Theosophists) or (b) the "super-physical" Soul Body or (c) an admixture of both. Which hypothesis best fits the facts is important: Apart from any other consideration, if man's total bodily constitution includes a "semi-physical" body (the vehicle of vitality) and a "super-physical" body (the Soul Body) then there are presumably corresponding "semi-physical" realms or spheres ("Hades") and "super-physical" realms ("Paradise"), as is taught in most religions.

The question of the nature of the "double" cannot, of course, be "proved" in a "scientific" manner, since "doubles," whatever their nature, do not consist of physical matter and cannot be weighed and measured. It must be decided on a probability basis: That hypothesis must be provisionally accepted which best embraces and explains all the known facts. This is, of course, the kind of "proof" that is usually available in our law courts and it can amount to virtual certainty.

Professor C. J. Ducasse,[18] one of the foremost philosophers of our time, made an important point: He drew attention to the numerous descriptions, by astral projectors, of a "silver cord" which united their apparently released "doubles" to their apparently vacated bodies and insisted that, if this is actually the state of affairs, then these "doubles" would not be mental images but "sights, fleeting but genuine, of something very tenuous but objectively present at the place where they are perceived." Now, there is, in fact, a considerable body of evidence that this is actually the state of affairs: (a) The numerous descriptions of the "cords" of astral projectors who cannot even have heard of each other are identical—some descriptions are by children and others are by illiterate natives; (b) several describe vitality pulsating in their own (or others') "cords"; (c) the circumstances in which "cords" are seen from released "doubles" are significant; and (d) the "cord" occurs in materialization phenomena —it is shown on photographs—and materialization phe-

nomena grade into the denser types of astral projections
(see Discussion).

Professor H. H. Price,[19] Emeritus Professor of Logic,
Oxford University, suggested that cases of astral travel
might be regarded as observations of, or operations with,
a subtle ("astral," "etheric," "psychical," "Soul," etc.)
body: that is, that the Soul Body is an instrument of
consciousness. There is much evidence to support this
view also. There is, further, much evidence that suggests
that the Soul Body is not merely an alternative to the
physical body but is our primary body for thought, feeling, and willing. If this is true, then the familiar physical
body is only secondary and derived.

Let us review the present position. First, in *The Study
and Practice of Astral Projection*[14] and *More Astral Projections*,[3] the analyses of case histories brought to light a
number of facts that cannot be explained on the simple
hypothesis of extrasensory perception (ESP) plus a
"double" that was mental in nature (either a mental
image of the physical body or an "archetype" in the
"Unconscious"). The first fact, as already said, was that
the testimonies of astral projectors include a significant
basic pattern of events and experiences. This pattern can
be readily explained on the hypothesis that these
"doubles" were objective—that they were "semi"- or
"super"-physical bodies. The mental image or "archetype" hypotheses need additional, hitherto unspecified,
hypotheses; for no (other) mental images or "archetypes"
have been described, conceived, or imagined to exhibit
such patterns. Thus both of the subjective hypotheses
violate the principle of economy of hypotheses.

Secondly, in the same two books our analyses revealed

that the "doubles" that were released under markedly different conditions (naturally, as opposed to enforced) showed constant differences: There was a greater tendency among the former to enter "Paradise" conditions, to see dead friends, and to have "super-normal" consciousness than among the latter. Thus, within the basic pattern of events and experiences, already noted, there are two subsidiary patterns according to the conditions under which "doubles" were released. These subsidiary patterns are also readily explained on the objective body hypothesis: In many natural releases, the "double" consisted of the "super-physical" Soul Body only, while in enforced releases the Soul Body was accompanied by some of the enshrouding substance of the "semi-physical" vehicle of vitality. Those who have advanced the mental image—or the "archetype"—hypothesis were unaware of the existence of these facts. Still other additional hypotheses will be required and the principle of economy of hypotheses will be violated still further.

A third point is this: Most who have studied the phenomenon of the "double," and who (we hold rightly) have felt obliged to accept the objective body hypothesis, envisaged "doubles" as entities which are similarly constituted in all cases. The present writer, on the other hand, holds that a few "doubles" (nonintelligent "ghosts" of living people) consist only of the "semi-physical" vehicle of vitality; others consist only of the "super-physical" Soul Body; and still others consist of an admixture of those two bodily features. Several factors determine to which of these three categories a particular "double" belongs: They include the nature of the release of the "double" (whether it was natural or enforced) and the total bodily constitution of the person concerned—such factors as his age and his state of health. Our hypothesis explains many facts that are otherwise bewildering (inexplicable on the mental image or the "archetype" hypothesis). For example, some "doubles" (those which include much of the vehicle of vitality) can move physical objects; while others (which contain little or none of that "semi-physical" feature) cannot. Some "doubles" (which contain very much of the vehicle of vitality) may not be able to pass through walls, etc.; while others (which contain little or none) readily do so. Some "doubles" (those with much content of the vehicle of vitality) have a "silver cord"-extension that is attached at the solar plexus; while others (those with little or no vehicle of vitality) have a "cord" that is attached at the head.

Fourthly, whereas the relevant facts so far mentioned have been brought to light by an analysis of the "doubles" that were formed in different circumstances (chiefly whether their formation was natural or enforced), in a subsequent study, published in *Intimations of Immortality*,[20] other facts were revealed by an analysis of the "doubles" that were released by different kinds of people. These included (a) those who gave evidence that they were of the mediumistic bodily constitution (with a loose, fluid, and extensible vehicle of vitality) and (b) by those who were nonmediumistic. Mediumistic people observed that their "doubles" included "fog," "vapor," "smoke," "clouds," even "water" that had left the physical body. This phenomenon was not reported by any nonmedium. We interpreted the "fog" as substance from the vehicle of vitality and maintained it enshrouded the Soul Body so that the relatively dim "Hades" conditions were contacted and consciousness was somewhat restricted or even dreamlike.

Fifthly, we noted in *Intimations of Immortality*[21] that the statement that "fog" left the body was made not alone by people (of the mediumistic type) who observed the temporary release of their own "doubles." A similar statement was made by people who saw the "doubles" of others that were in course of permanent release. In other words, the statement was made by persons who saw the process of death. Thus, Dr. R. B. Hout saw "a fog" leave a dying body (and gradually become its "double"). E. W. Oaten saw "a smokelike vapor" (which gradually became "an exact duplicate" of the person who had just died). Florence Marryat saw "a cloud of smoke" (which "gradually acquired the shape of the girl's body"). J. C. Street observed "a column of vapor" (which assumed the form of the man under observation). Major W. T. Pole reported "a shadowy form" (which became "an exact counterpart of the body on the bed"). Mr. "G" described "clouds" (which assumed the form of the body they had left). Maurice and Irene Elliott spoke of "a white hazy mist" (which also took the shape of the body it had left). Other instances are given in our Discussion.

Dr. Charles Richet,[22] a medical man and a foremost psychical researcher (who endeavored at all costs to avoid accepting the survival hypothesis), admitted, "The cloudy forms sometimes seen at deathbeds, as if an 'astral body' were emerging from the physical body, are probably not mere hallucinations." In point of fact, (a) pathological, nonveridical hallucinations are extremely rare with normal persons who are neither alcoholics nor insane; (b) in not a few cases such visions are collective, excluding the notion of mere hallucination; and (c) veridical hallucinations whose reality as monitions has been fully established are in all respects similar to those apparitions of "doubles." The fact that a number of these apparitions of "fog," "vapor," "smoke," and "mist" leaving dying bodies were seen collectively (in one case by five people) indicates, as Richet admitted, that these were objective in nature. The similarity of the various descriptions has the same implication. These phenomena were not mere mental images or "archetypes." What was overlooked though was the sequel: (a) In the cases described by Hout, Oaten, Marryat, Street, Pole, Mr. "G," and the Elliotts, these objective "clouds" or "vapor" were observed gradually to assume the form of the body they had left (and we have no reason to suppose that initially objective "clouds" can become subjective and imaginary); (b) the recognized "double" was then used as an instrument of consciousness—there were smiles of recognition, of farewell, and similar manifestations. In these cases an admittedly objective "fog" developed into a recognized ultra-physical body—one which, moreover, was a vehicle of consciousness. Richet failed to note that these people had not merely observed part of the process of transition; they had observed the survival of a Soul in an objective ultra-physical body.

Sixthly, these highly significant observations are concordant not only with those of astral projectors but also with others which were made by the persons who were themselves in course of transition. Dr. Karl Osis, Director of Research at the American Society for Psychical Research, published *Deathbed Observations by Physicians and Nurses*[23] a second series of which was reported in

Theta.[24] In the latter (much like Richet concerning the observations of phenomena like "mist," noted above), he said, "Two early investigators, Sir W. F. Barrett and Dr. J. H. Hyslop, found that the hallucinations of dying persons often consisted of visions of their dead relatives or friends. The second survey also verified Barrett's and Hyslop's hypothesis that the hallucinations are of this type." He continued, "The purposes expressed by the apparitions of the dead were related to the patient's survival [of death]. For instance, the patient thought they had come to greet him or take him to another world. This affected the attitude towards death of more than a half of the patients. When apparitions represented living people, they did not express a survival purpose and, as a rule, did not influence the patient's attitude. The hallucinatory experiences occurred predominantly in patients who were not under heavy sedation, who did not have an illness normally producing hallucinations, and who had clear consciousness to the end." *Verbum sap.*

Seventhly, we note the concordant evidence of numerous clairvoyants from all over the world, and covering many centuries, to the effect that everyone possesses not only a physical body, but also a "semi-physical" vehicle of vitality (given a variety of names) and a "super-physical" Soul Body (which also has various names). The vehicle of vitality is described as interpenetrating the body and extending beyond it for an inch or two (forming an inner and a denser "aura"), while the Soul Body is described as interpenetrating both the physical body and the vehicle of vitality and extending beyond them, as an ovoid, for several feet (forming a middle and a subtler "aura"). The true Spiritual Body interpenetrates and radiates beyond the physical body, the vehicle of vitality, and the Soul Body (forming a rarely seen "outer aura").

W. Whately Smith (late Carrington), one of the most eminent of British psychical researchers, in a book entitled *A Theory of the Mechanism of Survival*,[25] held that the facts of psychic science warrant the adoption, as a working hypothesis, of the idea that four-dimensional space is a reality and that the Soul can function in a four-dimensional body (evidently that which we call the Soul Body) independently of the three-dimensional physical body. Moreover, he considered that the "etheric double" (= the vehicle of vitality) is a connecting-link, or "bridge," between the Soul Body and the physical body. All these things were, in fact, said by numerous clairvoyants as well as being embodied in age-old Eastern tradition (being doubtless based on clairvoyant observation). Excellent accounts of the human "aura," with colored illustrations, were given by C. W. Leadbeater, the exceptionally able clairvoyant, in *Man Visible and Invisible*.[26] His descriptions, and the significance that he attributed to the various "colors" of the "aura," agree essentially with those given by Dr. Gerda Walther,[27] Eileen J. Garrett,[28] Phoebe Payne,[29] and many others, including a number of children who cannot possibly have obtained details from books, articles, or other reports. They also agree essentially with the descriptions given by people who had out-of-the-body experiences: for example, Sir Auckland Geddes's doctor friend[30] and Mr. Badenhorst,[4] an African native.

Eighthly, we have (although it is not coercive) what all scientists desire in addition to an argument that is logically sound (as in the above), namely, experimental evidence. Some "doubles" have been photographed.

In *Theta,* Dr. C. Tart,[31] when at Stanford University in California, heard of a woman who claimed to leave her body often and float up to the ceiling. He placed a card bearing a number (composed of five randomly selected digits) on a shelf three feet above her bed and asked her, when she felt she had left her body, to ascertain this number. EEG ("brain wave") measurements were taken while she slept. On the fourth night the woman reported having floated up to the ceiling and having seen the number: She called out all five digits correctly and in the right order. At the time she had this experience there was an unusual EEG effect (characterized by the alpha rhythm). The latter effect was also noted on four occasions during the first three nights when she felt that she had left her body but did not rise high enough to see the target-card. This experiment does not prove that the lady saw the number from a released, objective Soul Body (though that was, of course, a possibility); the correct reading may (or may not) have been achieved by clairvoyance quite apart from the release of the Soul Body.

Some people who have claimed to have had releases of their "doubles" have been able to produce certain physical effects such as supernormal raps and telekinesis (the movement of physical objects without physical contact). These, on our hypothesis, were people with the mediumistic bodily constitution: namely, a loose, fluid, extensible, and projectable vehicle of vitality. (Such people are not necessarily mediums and may, in fact, be averse to the exercise of mediumship—nevertheless, they are, by nature, potential mediums.) In the United States, Sylvan J. Muldoon stated that his released "double" started a metronome in a room adjacent to that in which his physical body lay. It also, on occasion, produced super-normal raps (which presumably could have been recorded on tape). In France, "doubles" released by hypnosis were made to approach screens that were coated with calcium sulphide; these screens were said to glow in a significant fashion. There are a number of photographs of released "doubles" (one of which I have heard of, but not seen, shows the "silver cord"-extension). A pendulum has sometimes been used to detect the locality of a released "double." Experiments such as these need systematizing and repeating. The best subjects would, of course, be people who can produce the "physical" phenomena of psychical research such as raps and telekinesis (due, we claim, to the "semi-physical" vehicle of vitality). Other subjects would presumably produce no such results. We cannot expect the objectivity of the "super-physical" Soul Body to be demonstrated by physical instruments. Never-theless, it can be reasonably deduced by analogy and from data obtained by the analyses of the phenomena men-tioned above.

In the following pages, we indicate certain other highly significant facts of astral projections. The cases are here classified primarily on the basis of the number of stages in which the "doubles" were formed (on our view, re-leased from the body) and disappeared (reentered the body): *Some "doubles" were formed (and disappeared) in a single stage; others in two stages. The point is that no mental images and "archetypes" have ever been de-scribed as being formed (and having disappeared) in two stages. Those who advance these hypotheses will be again obliged to violate the principle of economy of hypotheses.*

None of the nine series of facts, briefly reviewed above, has hitherto been realized by any psychologist, psychiatrist, psychical researcher, or medical man who has dealt with these important matters. All the facts are readily explained on the hypothesis that these "doubles" were objective bodies with two possible components: namely, a "super-physical" Soul Body and a "semi-physical" vehicle of vitality. We have offered explanations of the numerous and varied data on the basis of this hypothesis. Those who put forward the hypothesis that these "doubles" were subjective—either mental images of the physical body or "archetypes" in the "Unconscious"—are now under the obligation of advancing numerous additional hypotheses to cover these hitherto unrealized facts.

FIRST PART

"Doubles" That Were Released in Two Stages

"DOUBLES" RELEASED IN TWO DEFINITE STAGES, SOMETIMES WITH A DEFINITE TWO-STAGE RETURN

Facts:

1. In these cases (Nos. 20, 43, 53, 59, 69, 72, 73, 81, 97, 154, 225, 226, 244, 277, 382, 399, 408, 448, 449, and Edgar Cayce—20 cases) there were two definite stages in the formation of the "doubles" (and sometimes with a hint at a two-stage return).
2. The "doubles" were usually seen by the persons concerned.
3. The persons concerned were of a definitely mediumistic bodily constitution.
4. The persons were in good health at the time.
5. The "doubles" were luminous, subtle, and tenuous (not apparently solid).
6. They were used by their owners as instruments of consciousness.

Hypotheses:

The possession of a definitely loose vehicle of vitality caused these people to release the "double" in two stages: (a) a

"double" that was composite, i.e., that consisted of a significant portion of the "semi-physical" vehicle of vitality, which
represents the "bridge" between the physical body and the
"super-physical" Soul Body; and, since that "bridge" was
broken, (b) the Soul Body. This release from, or the shedding
of, the physical body was the (temporary) equivalent of the
first "death." The "double" was composite. Then an event
occurred which was equivalent to the second "death" of
"communicators," i.e., the release from, or the shedding of,
the vehicle of vitality that had hitherto enshrouded or enveiled the Soul Body. The "double" thus became simple—it
consisted of the Soul Body only. So long as the Soul Body had
been enshrouded, consciousness was restricted, sometimes
with dream elements, and the environment tended to be dim
(often with "fog," etc.) that was called "Hades." After the
second "death," consciousness expanded and was very intense
(with telepathy, etc.), and the environment was bright and
beautiful ("Paradise"). Thus, the "semi-physical" vehicle of
vitality of man corresponds to the "Hades" "aura" of the
earth; and the "super-physical" Soul Body of man corresponds
to the "Paradise" "aura" of the earth. The reentrance of the
released "double" into the body in some cases also took place
in two stages: namely, the reassociation of the Soul Body with
the vehicle of vitality (which was slightly dissociated from the
body), reconstituting a "double" that was composite; and
then the reentry into the body of the composite "double."
The facts are well explained on the objective body hypotheses, but the alternative hypotheses (that these "doubles"
were either mental images or "archetypes" in the "Unconscious") clearly need additional hypotheses: These have not
been envisaged, since the fact that some "doubles" are released from the body (and reenter it) in two stages has not
been realized.

THE FIRST STAGE— QUITTING THE PHYSICAL BODY

(*The First "Death" or Unveiling*)

PHENOMENA OBSERVED IN THE
FORMATION OF THESE
(COMPOSITE) "DOUBLES."

1. *"Fog," etc.* Muldoon[32] reported "a foggish light" everywhere and[33] stated that, at first, "everything seemed blurred and whitish." It was "as though the room were filled with steam or white clouds, half-transparent." This "foggy" or "cloudy" condition lasted for about a minute and then cleared up. "Reine's" "double" at first included "mist," "vapor" or "foam" that had left her body and collected above it. Collier's included "mist" or "haze."

2. *Dimness, darkness, etc.* With Lane the "light" was "subdued" and dim. With Professor J. H. M. Whiteman,[34] in an experience that took place in 1932, it was like "a dark night" (that is, there was a greater enshroudment of the Soul Body by exteriorized substance from the vehicle of vitality). Edgar Cayce described "fog" or "smoke."

3. *"Wind."* Frank Hives not only described "a thick

grey mist" but also "a mighty wind." Mme. d'Espérance
mentioned "a cold mist." Miss Marjorie Johnson spoke of
"cold air" and "a spirit-of-the-wind" sensation.

4. *Sounds.* Nancy Price felt that she (Soul Body) was
surrounded by "a web" (the enshrouding vehicle of vitality) through which she had to break, an operation
which caused "a sound like tearing silk." Mme. Bouissou
heard "a sort of silky rustle" which accompanied the
"skinning" process (the release of the composite "double"
from her body), after which she had to cross a "fringe"
(= "Hades" conditions) which exists between the physical world and the normal next world ("Paradise"). John
Lane felt "a gentle 'swish' " play, first around his feet
and later over his whole body until it reached his head,
when he felt himself ("double") rising from the bed—a
description which is often given by "communicators" via
mediums when describing what had happened when they
died!

5. *A confused, choking, stifled, oppressed feeling.*
These "fogs" and other conditions caused some (for
example, Mme. d'Espérance) to have a "stifled and
cramped" feeling. They were neither in the normal
atmosphere of the earth nor the finer and more exhilarat-
ing atmosphere of "Paradise."

(Our hypothesis in explanation of the facts just cited
is that the substances such as "fog," "steam," "clouds,"
"mist," and "water," which tended to obscure objects or
persons in the environment, and therefore generally to
darken the surroundings [the light being often "subdued"
and sometimes nonexistent], the "spirit-of-the-wind," the
"rushing mighty wind," the "cold mist," the "cold air,"
the "sound like tearing silk," and the "silky rustle" are all

ectoplasmic phenomena, indicating the release from the body of part of the "semi-physical" vehicle of vitality, and the "semi-physical" forces it transmits. The substance from the released vehicle of vitality more or less enshrouded the "super-physical" Soul Body—which corresponds to "Paradise" conditions—so that the composite "double" restricts the person concerned to "Hades" conditions, as described.)

A review of the past life. This was not recorded.

The "blackout" or "tunnel"-effect which accompanied the release of the "double." Mme. d'Espérance observed, "Everything became dark." D'nartsa "lost consciousness for a few seconds." Miss Marjorie Johnson "seemed to be drawn down a dark tunnel." Professor Whiteman felt as if he—the released "double"—were "carried . . . along the raised bank of a river." (Compare Miss Zoila Stables, who often felt like "going down a creek with high banks —or down inside a long pergola.") Mme. Bouissou went down "a narrow corridor." One of Lind's correspondents felt as if he were in "a narrow, dimly lit passage."

The conditions, or environments, that are contacted via these (composite) "doubles." Referring to an experience that occurred in 1950, Dr. Whiteman[35] saw "sandy-colored ground" which "seemed to represent a gulf between two spheres of existence" (between the physical world and "Paradise"—just as the "semi-physical" vehicle of vitality is intermediate, a "bridge," between the physical body and the "super-physical" Soul Body —"as above, so below").

Referring to another experience, in 1935, Dr. Whiteman stated that he saw "some substance like granite on a sandy beach near the water's edge." He also observed,[36]

"in transitional states between the physical state and a
psychical [Soul Body] one . . . there is sometimes . . . a
condition of shapeless fluidity. . . . Then in due course,
the new [psychical or "Paradise"] world and our new
personal form [Soul Body] are condensed out of 'the
waters.' " He added, "In these transitional states, mental
control is difficult, fantasy-influences sometimes take hold
and the separation [= astral projection] may lapse into
a dream of flying, floating or swimming." He observed
that the "currents" that eddied within his (composite)
"double" were "almost material in character—they could
easily be mistaken for physical sensations." Again,[37] he
mentioned a psychical sensation which he had felt at
"the solar plexus" ("about one to two inches above the
navel and perhaps two inches within the body"). This
is the point in the body at which the vehicle of vitality
chiefly emerges, and consequently the point at which its
"silver cord"-extension is often described as attached.

Still again, in Dr. Whiteman's experience of April 17,
1951, which, like that of 1932 already mentioned, began
with "darkness," discarnate "adverse powers" (the hinderers," who are among the inhabitants of the "Hades"
belt or aura of the total earth) tried to "possess" him, i.e.,
to use his vacated body, as in "possession" mediumship.
However, a discarnate helper (from "Paradise" conditions) came to his aid. In connection with this proceeding, Whiteman made a significant observation—the
helper had to "lower" herself to Whiteman's ("Hades")
level.

Edgar Cayce[38] described the release of his (initially
composite) "double" as follows: "There was just a direct,
straight and narrow line in front of me, like a shaft of

light [compare the "tunnel" symbol]. On either side of me [Soul Body] was 'fog' and 'smoke' and many shadowy figures who seemed to be crying to me for help, attempting to side-track me from my purpose [corresponding to the "adverse powers" or "hinderers" that were encountered by Whiteman in similar conditions]. I kept going straight ahead. After a bit, I passed through to where the figures were attempting to assist me ["helpers," who were in "Paradise" conditions—again compare Whiteman]. These urged me on."

Mme. d'Espérance similarly described "a misty, cloud-like region, in which one felt stifled and cramped, as though the atmosphere had become close, thick and substantial [again compare Whiteman's "almost material currents"]. Something in the vaporous mistiness, in the forms and shapes, recalled the dream-life [still again compare Whiteman]. . . . The longing to help these blind ones became intense [they were in the dim, dreamy "Hades" condition, earthbound, because the "super-physical" Soul Body was enshrouded by the "semi-physical" vehicle of vitality, i.e., because they were body-bound—the vehicle of vitality is part of the physical body, not of the Soul Body]."

Frank Hives[39] reported: "I am in a thick grey mist, with a mighty wind sweeping past me. Then I begin to see, through the mist, many shapeless forms. . . ."

In France, "Reine" was at first in "a thick black fog": It was "dark" ("Hades" conditions). She encountered jealous "hinderers," who "mocked" her and "held her up" by surrounding her released "double." They formed "a barrier" to her progress in the beyond. After passing through the equivalent of the second "death" (after she had shed the enveiling vehicle of vitality), she left "Hades" and entered "Paradise" conditions, now encountering definitely helpful discarnates. These "aided" and "carried" her "double," so that she began to see things on that plane, and that not by their aid (as applies to some trance mediums) but by her own efforts. "Reine's" contact with "Paradise" conditions was now so great as to be "almost equivalent to the after-death state." (But no mortal fully enters "Paradise," since his "double" is attached, by the "silver cord"-extension, to the body: On this account the Soul Body is incomplete. In addition, some vitality is passing down the "cord" to animate the body.)

Jeffrey H. Brown was, at first, in "mist" and he "mistook it for water." Mrs. Springer said that she "really stood on the borderland of the two worlds" (earth and "Paradise"). The Reverend Stainton Moses saw "the scenery of the spheres."

(Our hypothesis in explanation of the facts of experience just cited is as follows: These people had vehicles of vitality that were unusually fluid and therefore projectable from the body. This "bridge" being broken, the Soul Body was necessarily out-of-gear with the physical body. The "double" consisted of both the "super-physical" Soul Body and part of the "semi-physical" vehicle of vitality. Owing to the latter component, they first contacted the dim, cold, "semi-physical" "Hades" belt or aura of the total earth [which includes the etheric "doubles" of physical objects]. Its inhabitants include (a) the newly dead, who are mostly asleep or dreaming; and (b) others who are delayed in these conditions, the "earthbound." Among the latter are "hinderers" as well as merely weak and feckless discarnate souls. The enshroudment of the Soul Body by the vehicle of vitality not only makes the environment seem dark and misty, but also dims the reactivity of the Soul Body, so that consciousness may include dreams, fantasies, and hallucinations, and the person concerned may find it difficult to distinguish these from realities.)

The initial position of these "doubles." Muldoon[40] observed that, while his newly released "double" was near (actually within about fifteen feet of) his body, a distance which he called "the range of cord activity," it lay in a horizontal position above the body and the latter exerted a more or less strong pull on the "double," tending to draw it back into coincidence. D'nartsa's "double" was also horizontal at first; it lay some three to four feet above his body, which exerted a strong pull upon it. Professor Whiteman[41] stated that, in an experience of August 10, 1950, "Separation was in two parts. . . . At the end of the second part I [? = Soul Body] was raised high. . . . I was also aware, by double consciousness of another body [? = part of the extruded vehicle of vitality] . . . in a horizontal position." Describing an experience of October 1, 1949, Dr. Whiteman[42] included the phrase, "The separated form then appeared horizontal . . . above the bed." Simons's released "double" was "about a yard" from his body; "Reine's" was above; those of Miss Stables and Brown were above and lay horizontally.

(On our hypothesis, a "double" that includes a significant portion of the "semi-physical" vehicle of vitality [which properly belongs to the physical body and not the Soul Body] is body-bound. It cannot therefore get far away from the body and it tends to have the same [horizontal] position: "Double" and body, though separated by a few feet, are, in effect, a single body, because the "double" contains a significant amount of "semi-physical" matter.)

The movements of these "doubles." Muldoon[43] observed that (a) his newly released "double" began to "shake, reel, and unbind itself"; (b) his body "began to move, twist, and tremble"; and then (c) the "double" did the same so that the two separated, i.e., projection took place. *Thereafter (on our hypothesis) so long as the "double" remained composite—that is, so long as it included a significant portion of the "semi-physical" vehicle of vitality, rendering it body- and therefore earth-bound—its movements were identical to those of the physical counterpart.* Moreover, there was a strong tendency toward the mechanical repetition of various movements, reminiscent of the activities of many (though not, of course, all) traditional "ghosts" (discarnate souls who are also body- and therefore earth-bound). Muldoon[44] stated: "If you could observe the countless astral body activities, or astral projections, you would be impressed by one outstanding feature—while the astral body is within cord-activity range [i.e., quite near the body], this feature is repetition of movements."

This phenomenon of the frequent repetition of movements by those "doubles" that are close to the body (because they include part of the vehicle of vitality) is important in any consideration of the likelihood of the occurrence of the phenomena. The average person, on first hearing of the "double" and its temporary release from the body, naturally considers the whole idea fantastic and unbelievable. He has no memory of any such experience. But, as pointed out in *More Astral Projections*,[45] Neville Randall, of the *Daily Sketch*, who began his investigations on that basis, ended by concluding that, "It now seems impossible to doubt that such things happen often to quite ordinary folk." Muldoon found it "hard to believe that conscious astral projection is not universally known." Horace Leaf described projection as "very common." Staveley Bulford stated that it is "one of the natural phenomena of normal human life." Oliver Fox was sure that any who followed the methods he advocated would prove its reality for himself.

Mrs. Eileen J. Garrett insisted, "Everyone has a 'double' of finer substance than the physical body . . . the astral or etheric [Soul Body]." She continued, "This projection should be more fully understood, for I am always coming into contact with people who had experienced it and have been afraid to accept its significance. I believe that projection takes place more often than any of us realize, and that it happens very easily when we are emotionally disturbed, or when we are ill and the physical hold upon ourselves [= "double"] is less tenacious."

Yram considered projection to be "within the range of science," Phoebe Payne held it to be "perfectly normal." She said, "Shock and accident can momentarily drive a person ["double"] out of his physical body like an anesthetic." H. F. Prevost Battersby regarded "the business of the 'double'" as "quite ordinary." Rosalind Heywood[46] said, "Short of certainty, many of the cases are very striking." Dr. C. G. Jung observed, "The spirit world was certainly never an invention . . .; it was far rather the experience, the conscious acceptance, of a

reality in no way inferior to that of the material world."
Dr. B. J. F. Laubscher,[47] the eminent South African
psychiatrist, described many projections—some by people who could speak only Africaans—and observed,[48]
"The evidence of many people strongly suggests that
astral travel is quite common—except that few people
retain a clear memory of the experience." Yogi Yogananda[49] said, "Thousands of earth-dwellers have momentarily glimpsed an astral being or an astral world."

An American lawyer, S. A. Wildman, gave an account
of his "dream" in *Psychical Research*.[50] Among other
"dreams" were those of flying, of riding on a bicycle
"with incredible swiftness, without conscious effort," of
swinging (though realizing, quite clearly, there was no
swing); all these were such dreams as Muldoon[51] claimed
to be the early stages of astral projections. J. Malcolm
Bird, the Editor, in a footnote, wrote that these dreams
"are common to all of us and constitute a very definite
category of dream-experiences." He added, "I suppose
with most dreamers, as with myself, the most common of
all the dreams of this group is that of progressing in
prodigiously long floating strides [also mentioned by
Muldoon]. The attempt to explain this category of
dreams on the basis of race-history seems to me less successful than in the case of the 'falling' dream. Its explanation on the basis of subconscious desire is . . . not
wholly satisfactory, inasmuch as the desire for a more
birdlike locomotion can hardly be deep rooted enough,
in enough persons, to meet the demands made upon it
by such a theory." He concluded, "Where Mr. Wildman
says that he was 'in control of the movements and so
enjoyed the powers and was proud of it,' he strikes a

fuller common denominator with my own experience (and I believe that of the generality) in this dream."

A. Horngate,[52] on the basis of his own experience of projection, was "convinced that we probably travel much more in sleep than we recollect—unless startled awake."

Mrs. Muriel Hankey[53] had a spontaneous projection. She soon found that the art of quitting the body could be "cultivated." She and McKenzie then "met" frequently in their released "doubles." Mrs. Hankey could distinguish between true projections of her objective "double" and dreams, clairvoyance, and the like.

Now, these are instances in which the projected "double" was used as an instrument of consciousness. Such projections are extremely rarely remembered, and for a sufficient reason.[54] Our present point is that indicated by Muldoon and mentioned above: Many projections of the "double" occur in which one remains so near the body that the vehicle of vitality obscures and enshrouds the Soul Body, limiting, if not preventing, its use as an instrument of consciousness—the projections are more or less unconscious and no memory of them is possible. Muldoon[55] observed, "There are many, many people who are 'out' in their astral bodies, somnambulating, every night. But they do not know it! . . . *The world would be greatly surprised if it knew how common unconscious, and partially conscious, astral projection really is.*"

There are no sharp lines of division between these experiences, and to insist on the application of statistics to them is not wise. J. B. Priestley[56] said, "I am suspicious of the whole statistical method. Real people are not to be found among statistics." Dr. Alexis Carrel observed,

"In many cases the things that are not visible and meas-urable are more important than those that can be objectively selected and measured." Dr. Nandor Fodor[57] said, "The fundamental error is that we wish to make psychical research an exact science, that we are tempted to analyse psychical phenomena as we analyse chemical objects. . . . The truth is that psychical research can never be made into an exact science as it is basically a psychological enquiry. . . . Unless we shift the enquiry from the department of physics into psychology, we can only hope to find a few odd bricks from which no edi-fice can be built."

Another aspect of the movements of "doubles" may be mentioned. Walking is performed by very few "dou-bles" of the living (the activity, when it does occur, may be due to the force of habit—the "double" when interi-orized and "in gear" with the body, necessarily makes movements that are identical with those of the body). In the vast majority of cases, "doubles" do not walk but "float" or "glide." The "ghosts" of the dead, whose "doubles" include the whole of the vehicle of vitality, and whose attention is directed earthward, often walk (again doubtless from habit), and in some instances their steps are accompanied by sounds that are recordable. The floating of the "doubles" of both the living and the dead suggests their independence of gravity; yet they may be photographed, may exercise telekinesis, etc.; they are "semi-physical."

(On our hypothesis, a composite "double" makes movements identical to those of its physical body, and often mechanically repeats certain movements, because it includes much of the "semi-physical" vehicle of vitality and, though lying at some little distance from the body, is nevertheless bound to it: Composite "doubles," unlike those that consist of the Soul Body only [Second Part, Group IA], are not entirely free entities.)

When a (composite) "double" is released, and is near the body, the physical senses may operate, but, if so, they do so "capriciously." We owe significant observations concerning these matters chiefly to Muldoon.[58] He found that while his newly released "double" was within "cord-activity range" (that is, while it included part of the vehicle of vitality and remained near the body) he might have dual consciousness, i.e., he might see (a) physical objects and (b) "etheric" or "astral" objects. Although, as a rule, sight is by the "double" or "astral" body only (our primary vehicle of consciousness), "the senses can shift back and forth from one body ["double"] to the other [physical body], or be in both bodies and in the ["silver"] cable ["cord"] at the same time—within cord-activity range. . . . Oft-times the phantom ["astral body" or "double"] can be detached [within cord-activity range]. . . . The subject will see the phantom from the physical eyes, although they are closed."

Muldoon pointed out that this is possible because the observation was made via the "double" (the primary body). The observation passed along the "silver cord"-extension between it and the physical body, and stimulated the optical nerves. He drew an important conclusion from these observations, namely, that they prove: *"The seat of consciousness is in the Astral [Soul] Body"—that the mind, Soul, or Spirit is distinct from the physical body (the two being "bridged," as already said, by the vehicle of vitality). Again, "dual astral vi-*

sion"—which operates when the person concerned ac-
tually sees from the primary Soul Body and appears to
see from the physical body as well—also indicates[59] *that*
"the conscious mind is not part of the physical body but
operates in the Astral Body."

Muldoon explained the phenomenon just mentioned
as "a double-track sense of sight, one of these tracks
running across the 'line of force' [= "silver cord"-exten-
sion] to the physical body." He said, "The first time I
ever experienced this I thought it was dual consciousness [i.e., consciousness operating in two separated bod-
ies] but I soon discovered that it was merely dual vision."
He observed, "It occurs only within cord-activity range,
so far as I know." That is, so long as his "double" included a significant portion of his vehicle of vitality (and
was near to his body), Muldoon could see via his released
Astral or Soul Body. In addition, he sometimes seemed
to see with his physical eyes, even when they were closed;
this latter effect was due to impressions that were passed
on from the Astral or Soul Body, along the "cord"-ex-
tension, to the physical brain.

Turning to the sense of touch under similar circumstances,[60] Muldoon described how, when his "double"
was newly released and near his body, his dog jumped
up on the bed and pushed against his body. He said,
"The physical was rocked up and downward slightly
from the action of the springs as the dog's weight landed
on the bed, and the Astral, in exactly the same time,
rocked upward and downward in the air, in perfect har-
mony with the physical, although the Astral Body was
in the vertical, and the physical body was in the horizontal position." This rocking was, of course, also another

instance of the movements which tend to be identical, as between body and "double," so long as the latter is "within cord-activity range," i.e., so long as it includes a significant portion of the vehicle of vitality. Muldoon[60] wisely observed: "If you feel anything physical while in the Astral Body, you must be within cord-activity range, and what you touch will have to touch the physical counterpart: then it is transmitted over the 'line of force' [= "silver cord"-extension] into the Astral Body, and that is where you really feel it."

Muldoon[61] observed that, "A touch on the physical body may be felt in the same spot on the Astral Body," and that certain hypnotic experiments have suggested that the reverse process can also occur: "A touch on the Astral member can be felt in the physical member." For example, if the Astral Body is pricked with a needle some six to eight inches from the physical body, the sensation may be felt in the latter, i.e., there may be "repercussion of sensibility." He did not understand how a physical needle could prick a "semi-physical" "double." But our bodies can scarcely be the only physical objects which have "semi-physical" "doubles": If the body has a "double," so presumably has a needle or a stone. However, Muldoon insisted[62] that, "If repercussion of sensibility takes place, it does so while the phantom is within cord-activity range"—while it includes some of the vehicle of vitality. He characterized the latter condition as "a state of separation which is not perfectly free."

Others describe dual consciousness in similar circumstances, but not in the detail or with the understanding of Muldoon. For example, Dr. Whiteman[63] has a heading, "Parallel Consciousness in Two or More Spaces:

Mixture of Spaces," and, much like Muldoon, said, "These are features often (perhaps always) found in the beginning of separation [= the projection of a "double," which in his case, as in Muldoon's, often included part of the vehicle of vitality], or in transitions from one kind of separation to another."

(Our hypothesis, advanced in explanation of these remarkable facts, has already been indicated: The inclusion in any "double" of a significant portion of the "semi-physical" vehicle of vitality [which properly belongs to the physical body] means that that "double" is body-bound. Hence it tends [a] to take up the same [horizontal] position as the body, [b] to make movements similar to those of the body, and [c] to be affected by sensory impressions that are received by the body. It may here be added that such phenomena are never described by [a] those mediumistic people whose "doubles" have passed through the second "death" [the shedding of the vehicle of vitality, which returns to the physical body], or [b] by nonmediumistic people [whose "doubles" do not include a significant part of the vehicle of vitality].)

The "silver cord"-extension between the released (here composite) "double" and the vacated physical body. The fact that Dr. Whiteman felt psychical sensations at "the solar plexus" has already been mentioned: He felt "a jolt" there when his released "double" returned. Muldoon[64] described "a breath-taking sensation in the pit of the stomach" which was felt when his "double" was released on "a short-distance separation," i.e., within "cord-activity range" and therefore included part of the vehicle of vitality. He told his readers that this sensation was one of the signs of an "elementary stage" in the release of his "double." Evan Powell did not describe this portion of the body in relation to the process of release of his "double," or in relation to the process of its reentry into the body: He described it in relation to the "silver cord"-extension that forms when release takes place. He said, "I saw my own 'silver cord.' It was . . . attached to the solar plexus."

(On our hypothesis, the "silver cord" is a temporary extension which forms as the "double" leaves the body and which is reabsorbed as it reenters the body. Vincent Turvey, temporarily out of his body, observed, "This cord appears whenever the 'I' ["double"] leaves the 'me' [body]." This idea occurs in "communications." The "communicator" of *I Awoke*[65] stated that the "cord" "partakes of two natures," while that of Kate Wingfield[66] said, "The extension of the [physical] body and the extension of the Astral Body form a chain which still unites the two.")

The "cord" is described as relatively short and thick when the "double" is within a few feet of the body and getting thinner and thinner as they separate until it is like a spider's web (Muldoon).[67] When the "double" is near the body it absorbs much cosmic vitality, the Prâna of the Hindus; and this is transmitted, via the "cord"-extension, to the physical body. A number of people who had out-of-the-body experiences independently stated that they saw this vitality pulsating in their "cord." Thus, Muldoon[68] described "a regular pulsating action" in his cord and said, "When the Astral Body is in coincidence (with the physical), you are physically alive. When the Astral Body moves out of coincidence, you are physically dead—unless the astral cable, running from the Energetic (= Astral) Body to the physical body is intact. That is the purpose of the astral 'line of force'—to deliver the 'breath of life' to the physical body while the finer (Astral) body is projected." (This observation, made by an American youth, was made by others, for example, by William Gerhardi, M.A., B.Litt., the eminent novelist, who, out of his body, similarly observed, "There was this uncanny tape of light, i.e., the 'silver cord,' between us, i.e., projected 'double' and vacated body, like the umbilical cord, by means of which the body on the bed was kept breathing.")

"Communicators," via mediums, say the same: We summarized them as our Statement No. 20: "Until the 'silver cord' snaps, or in Biblical phraseology (Eccles. xii, 6), is 'loosed,' decomposition does not commence in the physical body. Until then, providing it is in fact, rehabitable, a man can return to and re-animate his physical body. Once the 'cord' is broken, however, return is impossible. Note that in the case of Lazarus decomposition had not begun four days after apparent death (John, xi, 39). It is said that the delay in decomposition until after the 'cord' is severed is due to the fact that vital currents are collected by the vehicle of vitality and transmitted, via the 'cord,' to the physical body. Several 'communicators' warn against cremation or burial before the 'cord' is actually broken—i.e., before decomposition sets in—since, in very rare instances (as apparently in the case of Lazarus), it may be a case of suspended animation."

Other people who, when free from their physical bodies, observed vital forces pulsating in their "silver cord"-extensions include Mrs. Gwen Cripps ("I could see the vitality in it, a pulsation") and Mrs. Clara Clayton (whose "silver thread of light" was "pulsating with life").

Others observed this remarkable phenomenon not in their own "silver cords" but in those of other people whose "doubles" were free from their bodies. Thus, Dr. R. B. Hout,[69] who observed the "passing" of his aunt, said, "As I watched the suspended spirit body, my attention was called to a silver-like substance that was streaming from the head of the physical body to the head of the spirit double. Then I saw the connecting cord between the two bodies. As I watched, the thought, 'the silver cord,' kept running through my mind. I knew, for the first time, the meaning of it—this 'silver cord' was the connecting link between the physical and spirit bodies, even as the umbilical cord unites the child to its mother. . . . The colour was a translucent luminous silver radiance. The cord seemed alive with vibrant energy; I could see the pulsations of light stream along the course of it. . . ."

In similar circumstances Miss F. E. Porter, of Hornsey, observed the "silver cord" of a man who was dying and stated, "It appeared to be vibrating as though a light were flashing up and down." It is surely significant that, as already said, this phenomenon was reported by Mr. Badenhorst, who described his "cord" as a "band" which bore "many spots of brilliance" that resembled diamonds. He cannot read English.

An obviously related phenomenon may here be mentioned. When William Gerhardi's "double" was free from his body, he said to himself, "Now to be scientific—this is one chance in a million. You must convince yourself so that nothing later will make you think it

was merely a dream!" He thereupon went to his flat
seeking evidence that would prove to him, after his return to his body, that he had not merely been dreaming
—he noticed which windows were shut, and other details. But he found that his consciousness tended to wax
and wane: "It flared up and then grew dim again." After
another quite clear period he thought, "How do I know
that I am not dreaming this? And the answer—look for
the lighted cord behind you." He continued, "I looked
round. It was there. . . . That satisfied me that I was
not dreaming but . . . my consciousness went out again
like a lamp. When it returned, it was so weak that I
asked myself no questions, no more than you would in
a dream. . . ." Then he was back in his body.

Mrs. Leonard not only described the same phenomenon but realized what caused it. When out of her body,
and after making a number of significant observations
which convinced and therefore pleased her, she said,
"Then I found myself back in my bedroom. Clarity of
thought was leaving me; I was less conscious, and thought
it was possibly because I was returning to my physical
body [the Soul Body reassociating with the slightly released vehicle of vitality preparatory to reentering the
physical body—the reverse of the second "death"]."

F. C. Sculthorpe also understood: When out of his
body, he observed that his consciousness was, in general,
more vivid than when in the body. "But," he stated, "it
seems to wax and wane according to the life-force reaching it through the astral cord."

Muldoon[70] similarly observed that, when his "double"
was free from his body, consciousness "may be inter-
spersed with unconsciousness, or it may never enter into

the act at all." He held that very many people release their "doubles" but do not use them as vehicles of consciousness. He stated,[71] "Just as there is somnambulism (commonly called sleep-walking) of the physical body, there are also persons who, while asleep, walk about in the astral body. This I have termed 'astral somnambulism.' It is a state of unconscious projection. . . ."

Whiteman[72] spoke of "fantasy" breaking into the clear out-of-the-body state. These facts support our hypothesis that any portion of the vehicle of vitality may enshroud the Soul Body—and the amount does not, of course, remain constant, so that the degree of enshroudment may vary.

"Reine," the young, uneducated French girl already mentioned, described her "cord" as "like a ray of light filtering into a room" (the latter being very similar to the description of the eminent English writer William Gerhardi). Collier suggested that, while the "double" is separated from the body, the "silver cord" supplies the "trickle charge of vital nourishment to the brain" (this Englishman's suggestion is identical with that of the American Muldoon). Dr. Simons felt the presence of "an elastic force."

The physical properties of (composite) "doubles." These "doubles" occasionally exhibit the "physical" phenomena of psychical research, making noises such as raps and producing telekinetic phenomena, "lights," and so on. Muldoon[73] told how his "double" started a metronome in an adjoining room: After it had reentered his body, he went and turned "the thing" off. Fox, on occasion, "could move physical objects without physical contact." The Reverend William Stainton Moses produced

raps, "lights," and other "physical" phenomena. Correlated with these phenomena, the "doubles" might not be
able to pass through walls. "Reine" could produce super-
normal raps, table-phenomena, and telekinesis. She felt
"cold" (loss of ectoplasm from the vehicle of vitality)
when so doing. Mrs. Howard Jeffrey, an uneducated
lady, described something "like white intestines" (vehicle of vitality) which left her body. She said, "I didn't
like to see them." Mrs. Joy's "double" could make raps
and exercise telekinesis.

(On our hypothesis, these phenomena are caused by
the inclusion of a significant amount of the "semi-physical" vehicle of vitality in the "double.")

*The effect of the direction of the attention on the
"double."* "Reine's" "double," when either composite
or simple, followed the direction of her attention (or that
of her mesmerist): She made long journeys and returned
with information that was later checked and found correct (that is, she exercised clairvoyance). Her consciousness was dim when her "double" was composite, bright
when simple. She exercised considerable foreknowledge.
Stainton Moses observed, "My will carried me along with
a peculiar gliding motion." Dr. Simons said, "At will I
could make the second body ["double"] lie on the floor
or move some distance about the room." Mrs. Howard
Jeffrey had telepathy and saw the dead—but also "earth-
scenes" (? or the etheric "doubles" of such). Jeffrey H.
Brown saw the dead: His "double" did whatever he
willed it to do. Stainton Moses saw the dead on many
occasions.

The level of consciousness permitted by these (compos-

ite) *"doubles."* Mention of this has already been made above. When the "double" of a mediumistic person is near the body ("within cord-activity range") and interpreted by us as composite (as including part of the vehicle of vitality), consciousness tends to be more or less restricted and relatively dim, to wax and wane, to be dual (to include the physical world), and the person concerned may find difficulty in realizing that he is outside his body. The latter fact was mentioned several times by Muldoon.[74] He said, "I believed naturally that this [released "double"] was my physical body . . . but that it had mysteriously begun to defy gravity." Many others failed, at first, to realize that they had (temporarily) left their bodies, and, according to "communications" from "the other side," many of the dead at first fail to realize that they have (permanently) left their bodies. They also suppose, at first, that the "double" is the physical body.

(On our hypothesis, this relative restriction or obscurity of consciousness is proportional to the amount of the enveiling vehicle of vitality contained in the "double." The amount is by no means fixed and unalterable, since the vehicle of vitality is fluid—part of it can return from the "double" down the "cord"-extension, to the body, or additions may travel from the body up the "cord" and join that already in the "double." The properties of the "double" and the level of consciousness it permits will necessarily vary.)

The repercussion and shock felt when these (composite) "doubles" reassociate very rapidly with the body. Muldoon[75] observed that, in these circumstances, "the physical body is jolted throughout—as though every

muscle in the body contracted at the same moment and
the body gives a spasmodic jerk, more noticeable in the
limbs than elsewhere . . . as a rule, immediately after
the repercussion, the subject is conscious in the physical
body." He continued, bringing the phenomenon into
the realm of common experience, "There are hundreds
of people, yes, everyone who sleeps, whose astral bodies
move slightly out of coincidence for the purpose of becoming charged with cosmic energy every night. Have
you ever noticed that, when greatly fatigued and in the
hypnagogic state, just entering sleep, you have suddenly
given a spasmodic jump and become conscious? The doctor calls it 'nerves,' but that explains nothing. The solution of the problem is simple. When the condenser of
cosmic energy, the astral body, is run down, the subconscious moves it out of coincidence as soon as possible to
enable it to recuperate more quickly. So, when fatigued
. . . the astral body moves out of coincidence. . . . A
sudden noise or an emotion, such as fear, and the astral
body repercusses, shocking the physical body—although
it might not have been separated more than a few inches
from it. . . . The most striking result of this quick re-
animation—when both speed of return and distance are
involved—is the feeling of being split through the centre of the body. . . . It is a sudden thrust of severe pain,
as though a sharp-bladed instrument has passed directly
through the entire length of the body." However, "This
more severe effect is not experienced so frequently as
'jumping,' for the reason that most people do not have
extensive separations."

Muldoon concluded this aspect of astral projection

with the following significant passage: *"Sounds, sensations and emotions cause bodily repercussions—providing the astral body is within 'cord-activity range'* [=
*providing the "double" includes a significant portion of
the "semi-physical" vehicle of vitality*]." He contrasted
this state of affairs with that which obtains when the
"double" is beyond the "cord-activity range": Then
(when the "double" consists of the "super-physical" Soul
Body only) sounds and sensations may be contributory
factors to the return of the "double," but the chief
causes are of mental origin and consist of emotions such
as fear.

Mrs. Frances Leslie, whose "double" left her body
when she almost died, gave a description that is almost
identical with Muldoon's: "I felt as if my whole self
were being split in two." Captain Burton, in similar circumstances, described "a tremendous crash"; Gerhardi,
"a jerk which shook me" and "a jerk which shook me as
if the 'machinery' dropped into my bowels weighed a
ton"; Mrs. Leonard, "a severe shock in the solar plexus";
A. J. Wills, "a jerk of the body"; Jeffrey H. Brown, "a
start" and "a slight jolt"; Mrs. F. Collins, "shock"; Mrs.
Reese, "a jump"; Mrs. Creven and Mrs. Frean, something like "a blow"; Whiteman, "a sharp jolt at the
solar plexus"; Lane, "shock"; Mrs. Twitterton and Dur-
ham, "a jolt."

(On our hypothesis, the very rapid reentry of the
"double" into the body, which causes shock, resembles
the severe clutch on a car. Those "doubles" that include
much of the vehicle of vitality repercuss most and are
brought about by physical noises and sensations; the re-

percussions—much slighter in extent—of those "doubles" that contain no "semi-physical" substances are brought about only by emotion, and especially by fear. Such "doubles" are presumably objective, not mental images.)

THE SECOND STAGE—
QUITTING THE
VEHICLE OF VITALITY

(*The Second "Death" or Unveiling*)

Phenomena observed in the second stage. Muldoon observed that the "steam" or "white clouds" that "blurred" his vision in the first stage of the release of his "double" cleared up after about a minute. Again, as already said, he found that his "double" was body-bound when it was within about fifteen feet of his body. With Evan Powell the distance was ten to twelve feet. With D'nartsa it was three or four feet. (Muldoon's experiments[76] showed that the distance was smaller when the health was poorer. He said, "I eventually discovered why the range of cord-activity varied. I noticed that when I was not feeling as well as usual the range of resistance [to the projection of the "double"], or cord-activity, was less than when I was in better physical condition. . . . The more healthy the subject, the more energy is stored in the condenser, the astral body, the stronger will be the flow of energy through the astral cable ["silver cord"]

—and the longer will be the cord-activity range. The more energy that is condensed in the astral body, the tighter will that body be bound to the physical counterpart. The more enervated the individual becomes, the less energy is stored in the condenser, the less tie it has on the physical, and the shorter will be the range of cord-activity. And if a person becomes weakened to a very great extent, the astral cannot remain in the physical at all—and moves out, sometimes permanently.")

In her first stage, as already said, Mme. d'Espérance's "double" contacted an environment that was dark, misty, cold (= "Hades"); then she felt "a sense of motion" (as the denser vehicle of vitality was shed and the Soul Body rose higher), which was followed by "increasing light" (i.e., "Paradise" conditions). Miss Marjorie Johnson felt "a rushing sensation," after which her "double" evidently became lighter, since it moved upward. Frank Hives, whose "double" similarly first contacted an environment that was "misty," also "began to rise" as "the mists disappeared" and he entered "bright light." Dr. Whiteman's original "sense of cold" and "confusion" suddenly "passed away." Then he contacted "utter reality" and thought, "I have never been awake before"—(he was operating in the primary Soul Body and in the "Paradise" conditions that correspond to it). It will be remembered that Mrs. Spaulding's original "double" evidently released "a seemingly gauze curtain," beyond which was "beautiful scenery."

Mrs. Piper gave several similar symbols in describing the phenomena of the second "death."[77] Among these are the following: "I [composite "double"] was carried into space until we came to a delicate blue drapery hanging in folds [= that part of the vehicle of vitality that enshrouded her Soul Body]. . . . We passed through it when it parted. . . . I then . . . saw a light . . . the whole earth was aglow [= "Paradise" conditions were entered]." Later, when her "double" was forced out by an anesthetic, she stated that she passed through "a dark veil . . . a long, robe-like black thing" which, nevertheless, was "transparent." Then "Everything looked so bright!"

Cayce passed from misty conditions, with "hinderers," to "a hill where there was a temple," with "helpers." One of Lind's correspondents described what seemed to be "a child's dress" (= his own enshrouding vehicle of vitality) which was wrapped round his "double's" head, i.e., his "double," as first released, was composite: It included part of the vehicle of vitality as well as the Soul Body. He "threw it off" (= passed through the second "death"), then he was able to get out of that room into a distant one, i.e., get away from his body further.

When Jeffrey H. Brown saw "mist," he mistook it for water and tried to pass through it (i.e., tried to pass through the equivalent of the second "death") and so enter clearer, "Paradise" conditions where helpers awaited him. He was surprised that the "water" did not wet him—it only looked like water. Mrs. Joy also went toward "water" and "tried to swim" in it. Mrs. Springer "stepped into the 'water' of 'a river' " and so entered "Paradise" conditions. She observed, "I would need no towel—my garments were as dry as before the 'water' touched them. . . ." She asked herself, "What has the 'water' done for me?" and answered, "It washed away the last of the earth life" (the last of the vehicle of vitality which binds the Soul Body to the physical). As already said, the case of William Dudley Pelley[78] is interesting in this connection: When his "double" (which we interpret as the Soul Body) left his body, it was naked; a helper told him to bathe in a "pool" of "water" and it at once became clothed. Pelley, like Mrs. Springer, observed, "The bath did something to me; what I do not know." (This process was, of course, the opposite of that undergone by Brown and Mrs. Springer. In their case a composite "double" lost its "semi-physical" component. In Pelley's a "double" that originally consisted of the Soul Body alone acquired part of his "semi-physical" vehicle of vitality.) J. Collier also described "water" and "swimming" in it. On one occasion he tried to get out of the tunnel (= vehicle of vitality) where he could see the "landscape"; on another, he seemed to be "swimming out of his depth"—but he stopped short of the second "death" because of fear. He said, "I thought I was in water and going over my head made me return [to the physical body]. . . . I felt in danger so there, fear returned to me."

Dr. Simons (much like Muldoon, D'nartsa, and others), felt "an elastic force" which tended to keep his (composite) "double" "only a little distance" from his body. He observed, "As the distance between the two beings ["double" and body] became greater, so did the elastic force seem to become more powerful. A limit was reached at which no effort of will could effect a further severance; this limit was about two yards." (Muldoon and D'nartsa, of course, by exerting their wills, did pass beyond "the range of cord-activity," did pass through the second "death," whereas Simons failed to do so.)

Various references were made to the second "death" in the writer's book entitled *The Next World—and the Next*.[79] In Virgil's *Aeneid* (Book VI, p. 388, Penguin Edition, trans. W. F. Jackson-Knight), the hero, Aeneas, plucked the golden bough from an oak, and, accompanied by the prophetess, entered the underworld ("Hades"). The passage continues, "As they approached the river Styx, the boatman ["deliverer"] spoke: 'This is the land of shades, of sleep and of drowsy night [= of dim and restricted consciousness]. It is a sin to carry anyone who still lives [in the physical body] on board the boat of the Styx.' The prophetess replied, 'Aeneas travels in quest of his father down Erebos's deep shades [the "dark" place between earth and "Hades"]. . . . You must recognise this bough. . . .' The anger in Charon's heart subsided and he turned the boat and came near the bank. . . . They crossed the river and disembarked on ugly slime and grey reeds."

According to Professor L. B. Paton,[80] the ancient Egyptians considered that the spirits of the dead, in order to enter the nether world, "Hades," first had to cross the sea. The Sumerian people of Babylon, long before the Jewish captivity (which was about five centuries B.C.), held that "it was necessary to cross the sea to reach the entrance to Sheol, the equivalent of Hades."[81] Thus Gilamesh was told by a goddess, "Deep are the waters of death." The Hebrews, to reach Sheol, had to pass through waters. II Sam. xxii, 5 (= Ps. xviii, 4) reads, "The waves of death compassed me, the floods of Belial made me afraid." Jonah, ii, 2-5, "Out of the belly of Sheol I cried . . . for Thou didst cast me into the heart of the seas and the flood was round about me;

all Thy waves and Thy billows passed over me. . . . The waters compassed me about." Paton,[82] like most, if not all, Biblical commentators, was evidently unaware that, immediately after the physical body is shed, whether temporarily (as in pseudo-death, or in astral projection) or permanently (at death) there may be some dimming of consciousness and some obscuration of the environment. Both are due to the enshroudment of the Soul Body, which is man's primary vehicle of consciousness, by the vehicle of vitality, which is not a vehicle of consciousness. There may be dreams and hallucinations and the environment may seem to be misty, foggy, cloudy, or even watery. The commentators therefore solemnly taught that those descriptions referred to actual lakes, rivers, or seas.

It seems certain, however, that the "waters," or "river" of death represented neither a particular locality nor the physical substance which we call water: It referred to a genuine, and a common, experience in which something was contacted that had some analogies to water. It also had some differences from the physical substance: As several of our deponents found, it did not wet them, much less drown them by excluding oxygen, and the experience was actually pleasurable. The place in which these experiences were undergone was the immediate, or denser, aura of the earth, a "semi-physical" sphere that interpenetrates the physical world and extends slightly beyond its surface. (The "super-physical" "Paradise" interpenetrates both the physical world and the "Hades" sphere and extends considerably beyond both. "As above, so below. . . .")

Many descriptions accord with that given by Virgil

(the greatest of the Roman poets, a few decades B.C.), the ancient Egyptians, Hebrews, and others; and many of them are in writings that have no connection with religion. President Lincoln, according to John Forster's *The Life of Charles Dickens,* 1872–4, predicted his own "passing" thus: "I am in a boat on a deep rolling river. I am falling in."

Thomas Hughes, the author of *Tom Brown's School-days,*[83] described an obviously genuine experience in his famous book. Arthur, who had been very ill, said, "I had really got the fever. I thought I should die. I don't know how long I was in that state. For more than a day, I know, for I was quite conscious and I lived my outer life all the time and took my medicine and spoke to my mother. But I thought time was over for me and that the tomb was what was beyond.

"Well, on last Sunday I [physical body] seemed to lie in that tomb . . . and I ["double"] was caught up and borne into the light by some great power, some living mighty spirit [a "deliverer"]. We . . . paused on the brink of a great river . . . and I knew that great river was the grave ["Hades"] and that death dwelt there [the shedding of the vehicle of vitality, the second "death"]; but not the death I had met in the block tomb [i.e., the shedding of the physical body, the first "death"]. . . . For on the other bank of the great river I saw men and women rising up, pure and bright, and they put on glory and strength [in the unenshrouded Soul Body, now in "Paradise" conditions]. . . .

"I tried to plunge into the river, for I thought I could join them, but I could not [could not completely free the composite "double" from its content of vehicle of vitality—though ill, he was young and vigorous]. I saw my mother and my sisters, the Doctor [Headmaster] and you, Tom, and hundreds more whom I knew, and at last I saw myself too, and I was toiling and doing ever so little a piece of the great work. Then I heard a voice say, 'The vision is for the appointed time. . . .'

"It was now early morning, I know, then. My mother was fast asleep [with her Soul Body freed from her physical body] in the chair by my bed. But it wasn't only a dream of mine: I know it wasn't a dream. Then I fell into a deep sleep and only awoke after Chapel. And the Doctor came and gave me the Sacrament. . . . I told him and my mother that I should get well—I knew I should, but I couldn't tell them why.

" 'Tom,' said Arthur, after a minute, 'do you see why I could not grieve now to see my dearest friend die? It can't be, it isn't all fever or illness. . . .' "

Coulson Kernahan[84] described how he "died." His body was in a deathlike coma for two days. He said, "I seemed to be sinking slowly and steadily through still depths of sun-steeped, light-filled waters ["Hades" conditions, corresponding to the vehicle of vitality] through which there swam up to me scenes of sunny seas and shining shores ["Paradise" conditions]." These descriptions of the second "death," first-hand accounts given quite independently of the "possession" form of mediumship, are essentially the same as "communications" received via the "possession" form of mediumship in which supposed discarnates described their own second "deaths." Moreover, the "communicator" named "H," as well as the mediumistically constituted Mme. d'Espérance and Mrs. Gussie Dowell, described the reverse of the second "death," i.e., the reassociation of the unenshrouded Soul Body with the vehicle of vitality. Such descriptions are readily explained on the hypothesis of objective bodies, but not on subjective hypotheses such as mental images or "archetypes." Clairvoyants give comparable descriptions. Thus, in Great Britain, C. W. Leadbeater[85] stated that, since "the etheric double" (the vehicle of vitality) is "not a vehicle of consciousness," it "surrounds" a newly dead man (Soul Body) "so . . . he is able to function neither in the physical nor in the Astral ["Paradise"] world." In America, Max Heindel,[86] who called this bodily feature "the vital body," said much the same.

In South Africa, Peter Richelieu[87] similarly said that until a newly dead man rids himself of "the encumbrance" which Theosophists call "the etheric double," and we call the vehicle of vitality, "he is suspended between the two worlds of consciousness" [i.e., between the physical world and "Paradise"]—he cannot function properly on the physical plane because he has no physical instrument, and he cannot function properly on the "Astral" or "Paradise" plane because of the clinging and enshrouding "etheric" matter that is represented by the vehicle of vitality. Later,[88] a discarnate helper was reported as having told Richelieu that he had been helping a newly dead man to pass through his second "death"— "he had been helping this man to get rid of his etheric vehicle, this being now the nearest thing to the physical life, the only life he understood." The informant continued, "Getting the man to make the necessary effort of will to disconnect the etheric from the Astral [Soul] Body round which it had wound itself had taken longer than usual." Still later,[89] Richelieu made a general statement concerning a man who, newly dead, was suffering great remorse and "would give anything to get back to his physical body." He said, "He often refuses to make the effort of will necessary for him to get rid of his etheric vehicle which had wound itself round his Astral Body at the moment of death. On account of this clinging etheric vehicle he is earthbound just so long as he remains obstinate and refuses to get rid of it."

Ruth K. Hall[90] nearly died: She saw *a stream of flowing water* ("Hades" conditions, due to the unshed vehicle of vitality) beyond which lay "a plot of ground" ("Paradise" conditions). She said, "I felt a deep sadness at having to leave this wonderful place" (and return to her husband and children). Peter Ballbusch (our Case No. 563) had a very similar experience when only five years of age: He described *a strange stream* and *a river* ("Hades" conditions).

A lawyer, S. A. Wildman,[91] "dreamed" while half-asleep (i.e., while his vehicle of vitality was partially out-of-gear with his body). "I was on the shore of a sea or lake whose waves . . . carried the fragment of something I was striving to capture and hold," he said. "Because," he continued, "I had not secured it more fully awake and the thought was in my mind that it was a dream . . . that I had been trying to prevent slipping away from me . . . [= trying to prevent its being "washed" away from the "super-physical" Soul Body by the enveiling "semi-physical" vehicle of vitality]."

The vehicle of vitality, in these conditions, clearly corresponds to *Lethe* in ancient Greek mythology. This was a "river" in the "lower world" (between the earth and Elysium ["Paradise"] of the early Persians). Those of the dead who "drank" of this "water" (in other words, those who were affected by the enshrouding vehicle of vitality) forgot the past. *It was mentioned as "a river" by Plato (Republic, x) as a commonplace belief (? experience).* The "drinking" of the "water" of Lethe was part of the Orphic initiatory rites which may be compared with Dante's draught (*Purgatorio, 28–33*): See J. E. Harrison (*Prolegomena to the Study of Greek Religion,* 1908).

It is surely significant that the supposed dead, who have left their physical bodies permanently, give the same descriptions (necessarily via mediums) of these events as those who left their bodies only temporarily, including: (a) people who had normal out-of-the-body experiences (e.g., Muldoon, Mme. d'Espérance, Frank Hives); (b) clairvoyants (e.g., Leadbeater, Heindel, Peter Richelieu); and (c) people who nearly died (e.g., Arthur in *Tom Brown's Schooldays,* Coulson Kernahan, Ruth K. Hall), all of which accounts were independent of mediumship. They also correspond to various ancient traditions, such as the Babylonian, Egyptian, and Greek, indicating, as Plato said, that the "river" of death was a widespread belief (and not a priestly "teaching").

"Private Dowding"[92] spoke of "the mists" ("Hades" conditions) which, he said, "hang over *the great 'river' separating your world [earth] from ours ["Paradise"].*" Like so many others, he stated, "All Souls must pass through these 'mists' on leaving their physical forms for the last time." Later,[93] he spoke of the clearing of "the thick mists" in the "borderland" between earth and Paradise and said that, when this work is accomplished, "the fear of death will disappear" and "Man will pass across the 'river' joyfully and unafraid." He pointed out,

"Materialistic thinking and the fear of death have separated our ["Paradise"] life from yours [on earth]: the
'fog' has shut out the 'light' and men on earth have lived
in 'darkness,' or at least in 'twilight.' " He concluded
with a very necessary warning to literalists and material-
ists: "This is, of course, symbolic." Still later, Tudor
Pole[94] quoted a man who was dying as saying, "There is
the sound of rushing 'waters'!"

Lord Dowding[95] quoted a sailor who had just died by
drowning (originally published by J. Dimsdale in *The
Triumph of Life Eternal*): "We were all drowned when
the tanker was hit. It [death] was very quick. *I suffered
no pain. . . . We were moving through deep 'water'*
["Hades" conditions]. . . . A stranger ["deliverer"]
joined us. His clothes were quite dry and he [Soul Body]
walked through the 'water' without it seeming to touch
him. . . . I said something to him about it.* It all seemed
so queer: we were going towards what looked like a sun-
rise ["Paradise"]. Then [after shedding the vehicle of
vitality = the second "death"] we came to a kind of
garden . . . then, very slowly, we knew we were what
we used to call 'dead'—but it was so different [from what
we had expected] that I couldn't believe it. We are in a
far better land than the one we left."

A series of scripts of exceptional value—the Cummins-
Willett scripts—was published in 1965 by Routledge &
Kegan Paul under the title *Swan on a Black Sea*. The
latter phrase occurred in the scripts in the following
passage: "Is there a swan [a Soul] that rises from the black
sea of death and flies away to other regions?" Here again,
the "Hades" region which has to be crossed on the way
to "Paradise" is described as dim and as having some

analogies to water. Obviously, such recurring references to "mists," "water," and "rivers" crop up so frequently as to be of unusual significance.

(On our hypothesis, the "steam," "clouds," "mist," something that suggested "a gauze curtain," "a dark, yet transparent veil," "blue drapery," and similar phenomena, which first obscured objects in the environment or even made it dark, [= "Hades"] and that caused coldness and some confusion of mind, represented part of the vehicle of vitality that, in these cases, had been released from the body in addition to the Soul Body, enshrouding it. The person concerned felt a sensation of motion and, as the "clouds," "mists," etc., were left behind, the now lighter "double" consisted of the unenshrouded Soul Body. The environment contacted was now light and beautiful, yet earthlike [= "Paradise"]. Consciousness was no longer confused and subject to dreamlike elements: It was very clear; there was a sense of "utter reality." This transition from "Hades" conditions to "Paradise" conditions described in first-hand accounts of temporary excursions from the body, independently of trance mediumship, clearly corresponds with the second "death" described at second-hand by entranced mediums, by "communicators" who described their permanent release from their bodies. How shall these facts be explained except on the hypothesis here advanced? These "doubles" are best explained as objective bodies, not as mental images or "archetypes." Such bodies, like the physical body itself, were presumably derived from [and eventually returned to] corresponding environments, conditions, spheres, planes, etc.)

The "blackout" or "tunnel"-effect which accompanied

the second "death." Muldoon observed, "There is a spot, just out of coincidence [with the physical body], in which, as the "double" passes upwards through it [shedding the vehicle of vitality at the second "death"], the conscious- ness seems to fade out to some extent [= the "blackout"], then radiates back to normal again." Miss Marjorie Johnson said that, after her (composite) "double" began to move upward (because it had shed the denser portion, represented by the enshrouding vehicle of vitality), "everything was blotted out for a while." Dr. J. H. M. Whiteman "seemed to be passing along black passages in a dream-like state." With Nancy Price the second "death" was accompanied by "a sound like tearing silk"; she then felt "a strange lightness" and saw her own body. John Lane felt a "swish," like a "wave." Mme. Bouissou seemed to go up "a chimney-like tunnel" with "light" at the top. Sculthorpe seemed to go up and out of "a big chimney."

As already said, Miss Stables, "after getting free from the body" (or releasing a composite "double" at the first "death"), felt "as if going down a long tunnel" or "going down a creek with high banks" or "inside a long pergola." Moreover, she observed, "It is too frequent not to have some corresponding reality."

(Our hypothesis: The "blackout" that takes place at the second "death" has the same origin as that which takes place at the first—during the brief period of separa- tion, neither the physical body nor the "double" is available as an instrument of consciousness. If the time is very short, the "blackout" may pass unnoticed; if it is rather long, the experience may suggest going down a tunnel or up a chimney.)

The conditions or environments that are contacted via these (simple) "doubles." During the first stage in the release of the "doubles" of mediumistically constituted people (or prior to the second "death"), the conditions contacted were typically misty, dim, confused, dreamlike (= "Hades"); following the second "death" they were bright and beautiful, yet earthlike (= "Paradise").

(Our hypothesis is that, just as a man's total body is not confined to the physical but includes an interpenetrating "semi-physical" vehicle of vitality [which extends somewhat beyond it, giving an "aura"] and another interpenetrating "super-physical" Soul Body [which extends beyond both, giving a still larger "aura"], so the total earth—or any other "heavenly body"—is not confined to the physical but includes an interpenetrating "semi-physical" sphere [which extends somewhat beyond it, giving an "aura"—the "Hades" belt] and another interpenetrating "super-physical" sphere [which extends somewhat beyond it, giving a still larger "aura"—the "Paradise" belt]. "As above, so below." Men whose "doubles" are released from their physical bodies—whether temporarily as here considered or permanently as considered on a later page—contact either or both of these spheres [and, in addition, sometimes glimpse physical conditions]. The environment contacted depends on the bodily constitution at the time. With mediumistic people, the originally released "double" includes a significant portion of the "semi-physical" vehicle of vitality and "Hades" conditions are entered; after the second "death," the shedding of that enveiling substance, leaving the Soul Body unenshrouded, "Paradise" conditions are entered.)

The position of these (simple) "doubles." Whereas the

(initially composite) "doubles" tended to lie horizontal and not far from the physical body they had just left, after the second "death" they became erect, though the body remained horizontal.

(On our hypothesis, the "doubles" passed from a body-bound condition, due to the presence of the "semi-physical" vehicle of vitality, to a purely "super-physical" [Soul Body] condition; they were therefore body-free.)

The movements of these (simple) "doubles." Whereas the (initially composite) "doubles" made movements that were identical to those of their physical counterparts, after the second "death" their movements were independent. Moreover, physical space meant little to them—to think of a place was to be there almost at once; to desire to be with a distant person took the "double" into his environment at once. Movements were now unrestricted in any way; there was nothing mechanical or repetitive about them as in the first stage.

(On our hypothesis, prior to the second "death" the inclusion of a significant amount of the substance of the "semi-physical" vehicle of vitality caused the "double" to be body- [and therefore also earth-] bound; after that event, it was perfectly free from both the body and the earth [with its "Hades" belt].)

The effects of physical impacts on these (simple) "doubles." Whereas, during the first stage of these "doubles," physical sounds and sensations could occasionally—and "capriciously"—enter consciousness (the bodily succession doubtless being [a] physical body, [b] "semi-physical" vehicle of vitality, [c] "super-physical" Soul Body and so to the Soul), in the second stage they could not.

(On our hypothesis, the initial "double" included part

of the "semi-physical" vehicle of vitality, which normally acts as a "bridge" between our physical bodies and our Soul Bodies; this partial "bridge" necessarily operated partially and therefore "capriciously." In the second stage it was not available; physical sounds, etc., did not then enter consciousness.)

The "silver cord"-extension between these "doubles" and the physical body. Whereas in the first stage, the extension was seen as typically attached to the solar plexus region, in the second it was attached to the head. Whereas in the first stage it was relatively thick, in the second it was thin, often like a spider's thread, and might become so attenuated as to be invisible. Whereas in the first stage, in certain cases, it was found to interfere with the movements of the "double" (some few got "entangled" with it) in the second stage it did not. Whereas in the first stage it exerted a considerable "pull" on the "double," tending to make it return to the body, in the second stage this "pull" was not felt. Whereas a number of people observed the pulsating vitality in their own "silver cords" in the first stage, while other people observed the phenomenon in the "silver cords" of people who were in the course of transition (the bodily condition being essentially similar in both cases), no one reported this phenomenon in connection with the second stage.

Muldoon[96] observed, "Once the astral body advances beyond cord-activity range, it is free and subject to its own will. There is no longer any liability to eccentricity of the senses, instability of body ["double"] or other complications which are present before reaching this superior position." He continued, "These complications do not disappear in an instant, but gradually, as the body ["double"] has been advancing; and, when projection eventually reaches a certain point ["cord-activity range"], the cable has diminished to its minimum calibre, resembling a long strand of spider-web and showing no activity whatever." He concluded, "Regardless of the apparent deadness or laxity of the cord, there is necessarily an intrinsic flow of cosmic energy from the astral, or animate to the physical, or inanimate; but this flow of force by no means compares, in quality, with what it was before this advancement."

(Our hypothesis is that the "cord" is a temporary extension between the released "double" and the vacated body, forming much as when a child takes a piece of chewing gum and pulls it into two pieces, with a strand in between, and being reabsorbed as he reconstitutes the original mass. There may be apparent exceptions to the rule cited above as to the point of attachment of the "silver cord," namely, that the extension between the vehicle of vitality and the physical body is at the solar plexus, whereas that between the Soul Body and the physical body is at the head. This is to be expected: Though some "doubles" may consist of the vehicle of vitality only, and others of the Soul Body only, many —including those of people with the mediumistic bodily constitution as well as anyone who is in the course of dying—include both the Soul Body and part of the vehicle of vitality, and the amount of the latter present may vary according to a number of factors, including health.

In fact, a number of people have described having seen what is obviously highly significant, namely two "silver cords," one attached to the solar plexus and the other to the head: That is, they were fortunate enough to see two separations in progress, [a] the vehicle of vitality from the physical body [with an extension to the plexus] and [b] the Soul Body from the physical body [with an extension to the head]. The first person to report this seems to have been Dr. A. J. Davis,[97] as early as 1868. He observed a man whose "double" was being released at death, and his name for what we call the vehicle of vitality cord was "vital magnetism" and his name for what we call the Soul Body cord was "vital electricity."

Major W. T. Pole[98] saw a friend in the course of transition and described "two transparent elastic cords" that united the "shadowy form," or "double," lying in a horizontal position, about two feet. He observed, "One body appears to be attached to the solar plexus and the other to the brain." [The "shadowy form" became distinct and "an exact counterpart" of the body on the bed; two helpers appeared and broke off the "cords" close to the body, and the process of transition was completed.]

"Myers," communicating through Geraldine Cummins,[99] said, "During sleep, the Soul exists within the 'double' while the body is recharged with energy. . . . The 'double' is an exact counterpart of the physical shape. The two are bound together by . . . two silver cords. One of these makes contact with the solar plexus, the other with the brain. . . . Death occurs when these two principal connecting-lines are severed."

Mrs. Gladys Osborn Leonard,[100] a medium of undoubted integrity who had out-of-the-body experiences, pointed out that some people state that the "cord" is attached to the head. She added, "Yes, I think this is so, but from certain experiences of my own, I believe there is also a connection of some kind with the solar plexus."

Dr. von Goot's drawing, reproduced by Muldoon and Carrington in their second work entitled *The Phenomena of Astral Projection* [Rider & Co., Ltd., 1951, p. 145] shows the two "cords." T. C. Lethbridge,[101] the eminent archaeologist, mentioned "two indefinitely-extensible cords" and added, "These were evidently known as long ago as the writing of the Old Testament: 'Or ever the silver cord be loosed. . . .' "

In *More Astral Projections*[102] the present writer published the testimony of Mrs. E. Iddon [who "knew nothing whatever" about astral projection prior to her experience] concerning her out-of-the-body experience which occurred on June 19, 1961. It includes the statement, "I awoke to find myself connected by two cords, one silver and one silver-blue, and in a horizontal position above my physical body. . . ." These matters clearly represent what F. W. H. Meyers called "undesigned concordance." They again emphasize the limitation of statistics to these things, without due allowances for our ignorance of all the factors concerned [in this case for our ignorance of the amount of the vehicle of vitality which may be present in a composite "double"].)

The physical properties of these (simple) "doubles." Whereas the "doubles" of people who have the mediumistic bodily constitution may exhibit physical properties such as raps and telekinesis, in the first stage, such properties are absent from the second.

The level of consciousness permitted by these (simple) "doubles." The "waxing and waning" of consciousness, its often subnormal, or dream level, and its occasional inclusion of dual consciousness (awareness of both the physical body and physical world and the Soul Body and

"Paradise" conditions), which characterize the first stage, are not found in the second stage: Consciousness is now "super-normal," with telepathy, clairvoyance, etc.

The reassociation of the "double" with the body. Whereas the rapid return of a "double" that was in the first stage causes repercussion and shock, that of a "double" in the second stage lacks such features. Moreover, in the first stage, return may be caused by physical sounds, but in the second stage it is chiefly caused by emotion.

THE FIRST STAGE IN RETURN—REJOINING THE VEHICLE OF VITALITY

(*The Reverse of the Second "Death": The First Reveiling*)

Phenomena observed. Mrs. Cripps, returning from an out-of-the-body experience to her physical body and becoming aware of her physical environment, found it "deeply misty." Dr. Whiteman,[103] in an experience of 1951, stated that it was as if he ("double") were approaching "a well of water." He noticed that the "water" (and the darkness) caused fear and said, "There came a vivid sound of rushing water in my ears and I awoke in the physical world." Percy Cole "turned away from the bright light" (of "Paradise") and entered a "gloomy tunnel" where "a stream of shadows" passed him. Hives stated, "The journey back to my body is the reverse of what it was when coming." There was "the return journey through the mist, the rushing wind and drifting wraiths followed by darkness [the "blackout" in consciousness]. Slowly I came to my [physical] senses."

Mrs. Piper[104] said, "I felt as if they were pouring something over me." Again,[105] when she saw a discarnate lady (who was in the Soul Body and in "Paradise" conditions) she exclaimed, "Something misty [her own vehicle of vitality] shut down over it." Still again,[106] after seeing her "dead" friends in "Paradise" conditions, she exclaimed, "A little white mist [her own vehicle of vitality] gathered over them and they're gone [from sight]." On November 17, 1902,[107] she described "a silk robe" as "swirling" over her (unenshrouded Soul Body which was returning to the physical).

(Our hypothesis is indicated above: These are ectoplasmic phenomena due to the "semi-physical" vehicle of vitality reassociating with the Soul Body and beginning to enshroud it. All the phenomena—the "mist," "water," "rushing wind," "drifting wraiths," and the dimness of the light—were described as occurring when the vehicle of vitality formed part of the "double" during the first stage of the release of these "doubles," as would be expected on our hypotheses; "Hades" conditions were contacted now as then.)

The conditions or environments which were contacted via these "doubles." As already said, these were "Hades" conditions. Whiteman[108] stated that, in 1936, when his "double" was returning to his body, "the light grew darker." He made a generalization: "This darkening appearance always heralds a necessary return to the physical world." In 1951[109] he again experienced "darkness" in these circumstances.

The penultimate position of the returning "double." Whiteman[110] stated that, in 1936, when his "double" was returning, it became horizontal at five to six feet above the ground. Then it began to be lowered into coincidence with the body. On a second occasion, in 1940,[111] and a third in 1944,[112] the horizontal position was noted. This horizontal position was also assumed by Dr. R. B. Hout's returning "double" (our Case No. 74): It took up "a position parallel to and immediately above" the body it was about to reenter.

(On our hypothesis, prior to reentering the body, the simple "double" represented by the Soul Body, united with the vehicle of vitality, became composite and therefore body-bound.)

The "silver cord"-extension. Muldoon noted that his "cord" thickened as his "double" approached his body, and vice versa. As Whiteman[112] reentered his body in an experience during 1936, Whiteman felt "a powerful tingling" at the solar plexus—then he was conscious in his physical body.

(Our hypothesis is again supported—whereas the "cord" of the Soul Body is usually attached to the head, that of the vehicle of vitality is usually attached to the solar plexus.)

The level of consciousness permitted by these "doubles." Whereas peace, security, and exhilaration characterize consciousness in the Soul Body, in the present circumstances there is fear (Whiteman), etc.

Repercussion. In an experience of 1954, Whiteman[113] returned "with a sharp jolt at the solar plexus."

(Our hypothesis is confirmed: These observations are the reverse of those made at the second "death.")

THE SECOND STAGE IN RETURN—REJOINING THE PHYSICAL BODY

(The Reverse of the First "Death": The Second Reveiling)

The "blackout" or "tunnel" effect which accompanies the reassociation of these "doubles" with the body. We have already mentioned Percy Cole's "tunnel" and Hives's brief "darkness." John Lane felt as if he were in "a passage or corridor." D'nartsa "lost consciousness for a few seconds" (and then awoke in the physical body). Mme. d'Espérance felt "a sense of faintness and depression" (and found herself back). Returning to her body, Mme. Bouissou said, "I noticed the same gentle rustle of the three sheaths that were felt when I left the body."

(Our hypothesis is that, while they were in course of separating, neither the "double" nor the physical body could be used as an instrument of consciousness. There was, therefore, a momentary "blackout.")

SUMMARY (Read Upward)

THE TWO-STAGE RELEASE (AND
RETURN) OF ''DOUBLES'' THAT
ARE INTERPRETED AS COMPOSITE
(*Read upward from bottom of page 101*)

Hypothesis:

These "doubles," when in the first stage of release from the body, consisted of a significant portion of the "semi-physical" vehicle of vitality (which, in people who are of the mediumistic bodily constitution is exceptionally loose, fluid, and extensible) plus the "super-physical" Soul Body—that is, they were composite. This meant that the Soul Body was in a more or less enshrouded condition, accounting for the facts of experience recorded at this stage.

14. "Hades" conditions were contacted.

13. These "doubles" were "earth-bound."

12. These "doubles" were body-bound.

11. The person concerned had dual consciousness, i.e., awareness of both "double" and body (and, through them, of the corresponding environments).

10. Consciousness was more or less subnormal, restricted, fearful, and variable.

9. At this stage the "doubles" made movements that were identical to those of their (vacated) physical counterparts —they were body-bound (No. 12) and therefore "earth-bound" (No. 13).

8. Consciousness was not steady and uniform, but often "waxed and waned" (because the enshrouding vehicle of vitality varied in amount from time to time).

7. "Drifting wraiths," "shadowy forms," etc., were observed.

6. "Hinderers," "adverse powers," and "mockers" were encountered.

5. There was a sense of fear, apprehension, uneasiness, repugnance, etc.

4. Certain strange sounds were heard ("a gentle swirl," "a silky rustle," "like tearing silk").

3. "A mighty wind," "cold air," etc., was felt.

2. There was little, if indeed any, light (it was obscured by the enshrouding vehicle of vitality).

1. "Mist," "fog," "clouds," "vapor," "steam," "smoke," even "water" were described: In some cases they were seen by the person concerned to leave his body and form part of his released "double"—the other part being the Soul Body. A "blackout" in consciousness was often experienced at this stage.

1ST STAGE IN THE RELEASE OF THESE (COMPOSITE) "DOUBLES" (= THE 1ST, i.e., PHYSICAL "DEATH") READ UPWARD

(Read upward from bottom of this page)
Hypothesis:

The Soul Body was rejoining the (slightly dissociated) vehicle of vitality: Hence, the "super-physical" Soul Body again became enshrouded by the "semi-physical" vehicle of vitality—"Paradise" was no longer contacted: "Hades" was recontacted.

5. "Drifting wraiths" were observed.

4. Certain sounds ("a gentle rustle," etc.) were heard.

3. "Rushing winds" were encountered.

2. The light was dim.

1. "Mist," "cloud," "fog," "vapor," or "water" was observed.

Hypothesis:

In the second stage of their release, these composite "doubles" shed the vehicle of vitality (an event that corresponds to the second "death" that is described in "communications" from the "dead" concerning their own two-stage release from the body). The "super-physical" Soul Body thus became unenshrouded—the dim, often unpleasant "Hades" conditions were no longer contacted and the bright, happy "Paradise" conditions were entered, with consciousness at super-normal levels, including telepathy, clairvoyance, and foreknowledge.

3. Helpers (and not mocking hinderers) were now met— much encouragement, help, and advice were received.

2. The environment was bright and beautiful—"a glorified earth."

1. The "mists," mighty winds, strange sounds, fears, uneasiness, drifting wraiths, etc.

(Nos. 1–5 below) were left behind, since the "double" was unenshrouded and the Soul Body was operating in its normal environment, namely, "Paradise."

A "blackout" in consciousness was often experienced at this stage.

2ND STAGE IN THE RELEASE OF THESE "DOUBLES" (= THE 2ND "DEATH") READ UPWARD

Hypothesis:

These "doubles" had returned to the early body-bound condition because the "super-physical" Soul Body has reassociated with the "semi-physical" vehicle of vitality: They were once again composite, preparatory to reassociating with the physical body. Hence, very rapid entry into the body (caused by physical stimuli, such as noises, as well as fear, etc.) resulted in shock and repercussion.

A "blackout" in consciousness was often experienced at this stage.

2ND STAGE IN THE RETURN OF THESE "DOUBLES" (= THE REVERSE OF THE FIRST, i.e., PHYSICAL, DEATH)

No mental images (of physical bodies) or "archetypes" (in the "unconscious") have ever been described as having appeared (and eventually having disappeared) in two stages. On the other hand, the facts accord with our hypothesis that these "doubles" were objective ("semi-physical" and "super-physical") bodies.

In a significant number of cases, the persons concerned described the temporary release of *their own* "doubles" as having taken place in two stages (first a formless "mist" and later a definite, readily recognized form). Their claim is supported by a surprising number of similar observations, made by *different people* who were under quite *different conditions*.

1. Two stages were observed *by others* in *temporary* releases of "doubles" of *healthy people*. The case of "A. G. U." is from W. H. Salter:[114] F. W. Rose, unknown to his friend, Mrs. "E," tried to send his "double" to her. Having rehearsed the journey mentally, he went to sleep with his mind fixed on the proposed "visit." The following evening Rose called on Mrs. "E" and learned that she had seen "*a luminous mist*" (first stage), which eventually turned into a replica of Mr. Rose's face (second stage).

2. Two stages were observed *by others* in the *temporary* releases of *very sick people*. In this case the "double" of a man who almost died was seen. Miss "R" and Captain "W" made a death-compact; whichever died first was to try to manifest to the other.[115] At a time when Miss "R" was in England and Captain "W" was in New Zealand, the Captain had a severe fall and was physically unconscious (= with the "double" released from the physical body). During that time, Miss "R" awoke from sleep to see "*a sort of mist*" (first stage) which condensed to form the head and shoulders of Captain "W" (second stage). The Captain actually survived his fall.

Delanne[116] gave a very similar case in France. Mrs. Stone lay "between life and death" (with the "double" released) for some weeks. During that time Mrs. Balston saw *"a light"* (first stage). Eventually "Mrs. Stone appeared in the middle of the light" (second stage).

3. Two stages were observed *by others* in the *permanent* release of the "doubles" of *the dying*. We have already referred to the "mist" observed to rise from dying bodies: This formless substance, which we interpret as representing the vehicle of vitality, underwent a second stage, one in which it assumed the recognizable form (replica or "double") of the now-dead body. Thus, Dr. Hout saw *a "fog"* which left his dying aunt's body; it condensed until it *"resembled the body" of his aunt*. Oaten saw *the "smokelike vapor"* which left a girl friend's body become *"an exact duplicate" of the girl*. Florence Marryat observed *"the cloud of smoke"* which left a girl's dying body *"acquire the shape of the girl's body."* J. C. Street noted that the *"vapor"* or *"cloud"* that left a dying man's body "assumed the form of the man." W. T. Pole observed that the *"shadowy form"* that left Major P's body "grew more distinct until it was *an exact counterpart . . . of the body on the bed."* The Elliotts saw that *"the white hazy mist"* that left a dying woman's body *"took the perfect form of the suffering one."* Mrs. Annie Brittain saw that *"the mist"* which left the body of a woman passed through a second stage and *became its counterpart*. Lily J. Price, J. P., of Australia, wrote and told me how, when present at the "passing" of a child, she saw *"a mist"* leave the head (first stage). She continued, "The mist gradually *took the shape of the* child's form [second stage]." Mrs. G. Vivian, B.A.,[117] saw *"a mist"* leave the body of her dying mother. *"It gradually took shape and resembled my mother."* Mrs. "Alexander" gave an identical description, as did Mrs. E. Herrick, T. E.

Morgan,[118] and an American literary woman.[119] The Reverend J. Lewis[120] saw a gambler die. A "mist" left his body and later assumed the gambler's form.

4. Two stages were observed *by others* when they saw *permanently released* "doubles" (those of the *dead*).

"A. G. U."[121] said, "After being in bed only a short time, my body ["double"] seemed to be suspended in mid-air. . . . I floated for some time and then *a spark of light* substance [from the discarnate "double" of her sister] seemed to come towards me until it resembled *a huge ball of fire* [first stage]. It came very close to my eyes and then burst, revealing the face of my 'departed' sister." The latter was smiling at her. The "double" was an instrument of the Soul.

Professor E. Bozzano[122] quoted a missionary from Tahiti who was told by the natives: "Shortly after a human body ceases to breathe, *a vapor* rises from the head [first stage] . . . this vapor gradually . . . *assumes the form of the inert body* [second stage]."

Mrs. Leonard[123] saw *"a circular patch of light."* Later, "In this 'light' I saw *my [newly dead] mother."* In France, "Reine"[124] saw *"a blue light"* which transformed itself into *"a head and shoulders."* Remilleo[125] saw a *"light"* and later, in it, *"a human being."*

"Kenwood's"[126] wife was ill and he retired to bed exhausted (under which condition part of the vehicle of vitality would be released). He said, "My spirit ["double"—here composite] left my body, which I saw. . . . I saw a 'star' [first stage] which came nearer and, in passing, *assumed the head, neck and thorax* of my [deceased] grandfather" [second stage].

Mrs. "V" awoke in India with a sensation "as if half

her life [ectoplasm from the vehicle of vitality] had been taken" from her. She saw *"lights" which gave place to a "cloud"* and "after a few moments," she said, *"the face of a dear sister* then living (as I believed) appeared in the 'cloud.'" It transpired that the sister had, in fact, died that night in London.[127]

Mr. Davis,[128] in Florence, awoke and saw *a "light"*: "Immediately *a figure appeared,* approached the bed and leaned over as if to kiss me." The features were those of his dead mother. The "double" fulfilled a purpose. Horace Traubel[129] saw *a "light"* which "took the likeness of Walt Whitman." The latter gave him "a kindly re-assuring smile."

F. W. Fitzsimons[130] saw *"a small luminous ball."* Then the face of his (discarnate) mother appeared in it.

A. V. Burton, a freethinker, of Nairobi, Kenya, wrote (*in litt.*): "I had pneumonia and was apparently 'passing away.' I went into a coma [because a large portion of the "semi-physical" "bridge" between the physical and Soul bodies was ejected]." He later "came to" and "saw the heads of three friends who had 'passed away.'" He made the following significant observation: "When I first saw them, 'life' was pouring out of my body like electricity."

5. Two stages were observed by *investigators* when certain "materializations" were formed.

Nandor Fodor,[131] in England, described a materialization as beginning in *"a floating flame"* and later becoming *a recognizable figure.* René Sudre,[132] in France, observed, "One first sees *'lights'* appearing—there then forms *a mass* of *cloudy matter,* phosphorescent, and finally taking *the shape of a veritable human form*—alive and speaking." In Norway, Judge Dahl[133] observed, "There oozed from the cabinet . . . *a column of mist*. Gradually it became more sharply outlined. . . . *It was recognized . . . as a deceased relative*."

6. Two stages were observed by *"communicators"* who saw *permanent* release of "doubles," i.e., *death* (these accounts, via mediums, agreeing with those given by mortals independently of mediums—Nos. 3 and 4).

In America, Mrs. Longley's "communicator"[134] said that *"mist"* left a dying body and that it "gradually assumed *a complete resemblance to the woman on the bed*." In England, the Reverend C. L. Tweedale's[135] "communicator" said that *"light"* left a body and "became *a replica of the body"*; while J. J. Morse[136] was told that *"a luminous sphere"* left a body and *"gradually assumed the form of the person who had died*."

7. Just as mediumistic people observed that the *release* of their own "doubles" was a two-stage process, so they observed that their *reentrance* into the body was a two-stage process (see Summary).

Three points may here be made. First, in all the varying circumstances of both the seer (whether mortal or discarnate) and the period of discarnation (whether temporary or permanent) and the condition of the person concerned (whether well, ill, or dying), the "mist," "fog," "vapor," "smoke," "light," etc., described refers clearly to the "semi-physical" vehicle of vitality.

Secondly, those mediumistically constituted persons who described a two-stage release in their own out-of-the-body experiences (cited in the First Part) also described a two-stage return.

Thirdly, these deponents, although unaware that their

testimonies contained details which can be checked by the process of comparative analysis, are clearly vindicated by that process. There is no reasonable doubt that they told the simple truth. The same applies to the testimonies concerning the conditions under which numerous deponents described having seen their own "silver cord"-extensions: Those who said that their "doubles" were *above the body* went on to say that they saw the "cord" when they *"looked down."* Those who said that they had erected and were *moving away from the body* went on to say that they saw the "cord" when they *"turned round."*

SECOND PART

"Doubles" That Were Released
in One Stage and with a
Single-Stage Return

Facts:

1. In these cases (Nos. 40–42, 46–52, 56–58, 60–68, 70–71, 74–80, 82–83, 85–96, 98–119, 161–224, 227–43, 245–48, 250–53, 255–57, 259–76, 276–85, 386, 388–91, 394, 419, 425, 447, 450, 455—197 cases) the "doubles" formed (and eventually disappeared) in a single stage.
2. The "doubles" were usually seen by the persons concerned (occasionally by others).
3. The persons concerned were presumably of the non-mediumistic type—there is no evidence of mediumicity.
4. They were in good health at the time.
5. The "doubles" were luminous, subtle, and tenuous (rather than apparently solid and dense). In most cases there was a one-stage release (the "double" remaining simple—Soul Body only).
6. They were used by their owners as instruments of consciousness.

Hypotheses:

The people who comprise this group release "doubles" that consist of the Soul Body only, and they do this more or less readily because they are of a more or less high spiritual development—the high thinking and feeling make the Soul Body "vibrate" at high rates of speed so that it remains associated ("in gear") with the sluggish physical body only with difficulty. Spiritual development tends to cause this kind of projection; and the help and instruction that may be received during such "visits" to the "Paradise" aura of the earth, with its willing, wise, and able helpers, further advance spirituality: "To him that hath shall be given"—Matt. xiii, 12. (Details of such help and instruction seldom, if ever, enter normal, i.e., brain consciousness.) Mediumistically constituted people release "doubles" that consist of the Soul Body plus part of the vehicle of vitality. They also more or less readily project their "doubles"; but the cause is a bodily one, not a mental and spiritual one: Mediumistic people (First Part) may be spiritual or they may not. Since they have a particularly fluid and extensible vehicle of vitality, part of it readily leaves the body, especially under the stress of emotion, great fatigue, or the strong direction of the attention. This means that the "bridge" between the "super-physical" Soul Body and the physical body partly breaks, necessarily separating the Soul Body from the physical: A complete "double" is released—and this usually passes through the second "death," leaving the Soul Body unenshrouded. Yram and Professor Whiteman are evidently both highly spiritual and mediumistic. Others may be gross and mediumistic, while there are naturally all gradations between these two extremes. *It is the gross-and-mediumistic people who have brought psychic matters into disrepute.* All, whether aware of it or not, receive the kind of "help" they want, and therefore deserve. A person who tends, at first, merely to exaggerate may well end with deliberate lies or despicable fraud. Many observers have argued from the particular to the general and concluded that all psychic activities and phenomena are necessarily evil.

GROUP IA.
"SUPER-PHYSICAL"
(*Soul Body*) "DOUBLES"

Phenomena observed in the formation of these "doubles." A dozen or more of these people observed that their "doubles" left their bodies via the head. Others, who failed to observe (or to record) the actual release of their "doubles," nevertheless did observe that the "silver cord"-extension was attached to the head (see below, under "The silver cord"). None of these deponents produced "super-normal" raps, or reported seeing "mist," "fog," or "clouds" leave their bodies to form part of their "doubles"—that is, none of them showed signs of possessing the mediumistic bodily constitution.

(On our hypothesis, in these cases it was the "super-physical" Soul Body only that was released from the physical body.)

The review of the past life. Gerhardi and Hume each reported experiencing a nonemotional review of his past life.

(On our hypothesis, the vehicle of vitality as well as the brain is modified by, and therefore bears a record of, the past life. The separation of the "double" from the body may therefore cause this review.)

The "blackout" or "tunnel"-effect which accompanies the release of the "double." Sigrid Kaeyer, who experienced "a moment's blackness," made the following significant observation: "The 'blackness' of unconsciousness was just long enough for my Soul [Body] to escape from the physical." Lind, Miss Okeden, Mrs. Bounds, and Miss Bazett all mentioned "a tunnel." Lind also used the phrase "a dimly lit passage." Mrs. Boorman described "a stillness," and Rene C. "a momentary clouding of consciousness." Funk became "unconscious for an instant." Dennis and Mrs. Burles heard "a click."

(On our hypothesis, the "blackout" or "tunnel"-effect is due to the fact that, while the "double" is in process of separating from the body, neither was available as an instrument of consciousness—much as, when we change gears in a motor car, there is a brief lapse in the transmission of power. When a "double" is released very rapidly, the "blackout" may be so brief as to pass unnoticed, or may be so slight as to be unremembered; if the process is relatively slow, on the other hand, it may seem like going down a dark tunnel, or along a corridor or a passage.)

The conditions, or environments, that are contacted via these "doubles." Many of these people recorded contacting the physical world, though it may have been the (indistinguishable) etheric doubles of physical objects. It should be remembered that these cases necessarily include a number of projections that did not go beyond a very early stage. Descriptions of "Paradise" conditions were given by Newby ("another world"), Kaeyer ("a new world of people—the dead"), Hout ("a new but very natural environment"), Pelley ("a locality where persons I had always called 'dead' were not dead but very much alive"), Bennett ("super-terrestrial dimensions"), Fisher ("lovely scenery" with "people dressed in white"), the "Prodigal" ("spirit-life as it will be when free from the flesh"), Snell ("a scene of wondrous beauty—a vast parklike garden, and the light there is a light that never was seen on sea or land"), Henderson ("the most beautiful scenery ever seen"), Crane, Addison, Miss "W. S.," Sculthorpe, etc. A few described both "Paradise" and earth (or the indistinguishable etheric double) conditions—they were Larsen, Davis-Neel, Bulford, and Mrs. Cripps. None of these people encountered discarnate hinderers (as did mediumistic people). On the contrary, many reported having received help to leave their bodies, help to make observations when free from them, advice on when to return, etc. Again, these deponents did not report seeing the "mist," "fog," etc.—a feature that characterizes the accounts of mediumistic people.

Many, who saw dead friends, must have glimpsed "Paradise" conditions: They were Miss Peters, J. H. Dennis, Mrs. Sheridan, Edwards, Wirt, Gilbert, Kaeyer, Pelley, Griggs, Dixon, Red Indian, Stead, Snell, Sheppard, Mytton-Hill, Emerson, Eshelby, Graham, Mayo, Latham, Herrick, Swedenborg, and Mr. Serrano's sister.

(On our hypothesis, these deponents released a "double" that was simple, one that consisted of the "superphysical" Soul Body only: The latter was not enveiled or enshrouded by any significant part of the substance of the "semi-physical vehicle of vitality." These people did not therefore contact the relatively dim and often "misty" "Hades" conditions.)

The initial position of the "double." A number described their newly released "doubles" as occupying a remarkable position, namely horizontal, just above the vacated body. They were J. McCormack (who noted "this rather odd position"), Miss Bazett (about three feet above), Mrs. C. H. Smith (about a foot above), Mulvey (about three feet above), Dennis, Mr. "H," Mrs. Boorman, Dr. Gilbert, Mrs. Hibberd, Miss Douglas, Nurse Normanby, Mrs. "Horam," Miss Dean, G. Lester, and Mrs. Folson (*when she was a child of five or six years*). More than a score of others, who did not describe the horizontal position, did note that their "doubles" were above their bodies.

(On our interpretation, those "doubles" that remained quite near to, and parallel to, the body they had just left, were still somewhat affected by it: This might be the result of habitual thoughts—many failed, at first, to realize that they were not in the physical body. On the other hand, some of the "doubles" may have temporarily included a tincture of the "semi-physical" vehicle of vitality.

As we interpret the evidence, these "doubles" were not body-bound and therefore not earth-bound, and this was because they included little, if indeed any, of the "semi-physical" vehicle of vitality.)

The physical senses. The physical senses did not affect these "doubles."

The "silver cord"-extension between the released "double" and the vacated body.

1. Simple terms. The word *"cord"* was used by Mrs. Argles, Mrs. May, Mrs. Harris, Ibbetson and Edwards (attached to head), Urquhart ("near the navel—like an umbilical cord"), Keane (whose "cord" was "smoky, silver-color and about a half to three-eighths of an inch thick"), Goddard ("a band like a cord"—to the head), and Mrs. Helm ("a slight cord").

"Ribbon" was used by Mrs. Matile ("a greasy-like ribbon") and Moss ("a long ribbon"—to the head).

"String" was used by three deponents, by Mrs. Doan, Mrs. "T. D." (a "smoky string"—compare Keane above), and Mrs. Folson (who made the observation when a child of five to six years of age—"a sort of lustrous 'kite-string,' as I called it in my mind").

"Pipe line" was the term used by Mrs. Hutchinson, "a kind of pipe line" (which guided her released "double" back to her vacated body).

2. Descriptive terms.

(a) A *"silver cord"* was used by Lester; Wirt spoke of "a silver cord or chain"; Mrs. Gilbert, "a cloudy-looking cord"; the Tibetans, "an almost impalpable cord."

(b) Luminosity emphasized—Mrs. Williams, "a shining white cord" (to the head); Mrs. Herrick, "a long cord or streamer of light"; Mrs. Clayton, "a silver thread of light which pulsated with life"; McGreery's child informant, "a sunbeam" (down which she "slid" back to her body).

(On our hypothesis, these "cords" are extensions between the released Soul Body and the vacated physical body: The released "double" is not quite complete, while the vacated body is not entirely vacated.)

The physical properties of these "doubles." These

were nonexistent: *The "doubles" were "super-physical."*
There are no accounts of raps or telekinesis (as there are
in cases of the "semi-physical" "doubles" of mediumistic
people). The projectors (for example, Funk, Moss, and
Mrs. Herrick) passed through walls and other barriers
without hindrance.

*The effect of the direction of the attention in the
"doubles."* The "doubles" immediately and automatically responded to the direction of their owners' attention: They were not affected by physical space (as were
their physical counterparts). Thus Gibier's engraver,
when freed from his body, "had hardly conceived" a
wish to be in the room of a neighbor, when his "double"
was there. S. R. Wilmot's wife, in England, was "extremely anxious" about her husband, who was a thousand miles away crossing the Atlantic: Her released
"double" visited him. Moreover, a fellow passenger of
her husband saw the lady's "double." This case was
well attested. Mrs. Newby found her "double" free from
her body, and lying near it. She said, "I no sooner
thought of getting up than I was in the center of the
room." Miss Okeden, on several occasions, was anxious
concerning a friend: Each time she found herself, in the
released "double," with that friend. Another person
(Case No. 119) "thought of a friend" and "at once"
found himself with the friend. The attention of Mrs.
Muriel Hankey was directed to her friend Hewat Mc-
Kenzie, since she wished to tell him of her troubles:
Her "double" became released, and at once went to him.
He saw it. The Reverend William Stainton Moses, with
his "double" released from his body, observed, "My will

carried me along with a peculiar gliding motion." These are all instances of going away from the body. Mrs. Clara Clayton, when out of her physical body, wished to return: She observed, "Swift as the thought had come, I was back in it."

This matter of the "double," once released from enmeshment in its physical counterpart, responding immediately and automatically to the direction of the attention could scarcely be imagined and is clearly significant. Writing in 1966, John Vyvyan[137] noted that there are at least sixteen successful cases of people who willed, before going to sleep, to appear to a friend, and in some their released "doubles" were quite unexpectedly seen by that friend,[138] and that the spontaneous direction of the attention during waking hours (e.g., Miss Jackson)[139] had the same effect (see also the cases which we place in our Group I B, those in which the "double" consists of the vehicle of vitality only). Vyvyan said, "The curious conclusion to which this part of the evidence seems to be driving is that wherever thought is directed to a particular person or place, the thinker is, to some extent, psychically present [in the "double"] and observable there."

In this connection it is interesting to note that, nearly a century ago, Mrs. Cora L. V. Tappan,[140] a woman whose only education consisted of "the three R's" at a village school, received the following "communication": "It is possible to satisfy yourself on the existence of the 'double.' . . . If you intently think of a distant person, and at the same time figure his appearance to your imagination . . . to a certain extent your spirit

[in the "double"] is really there, and that friend, were
he a sensitive and impressionable person, could detect
your presence ["double"] in the atmosphere."

This important matter can be taken further: In addition to that noted by Vyvyan (the direction of the attention during waking hours and its deliberate direction
prior to entering sleep), there are several others.

3. In Vyvyan's two categories (additional examples of
which were contributed to the *Journal of the Society for
Psychical Research*, 1965 and 1966, by the present
writer), the "double" is not used as an instrument of
consciousness, and the projector is unaware that it is
released from his body; but in the cases we have cited
above both of these desiderata are present.

4. The direction of the attention of the dying, chiefly
toward loved ones who have predeceased them, an operation which in *The Supreme Adventure* we described
as "the call," is another case in point. Moreover, this
"call" is almost invariably based on affection. "Calls"
are commonly followed by "deathbed vision" or "meeting cases," i.e., by reciprocal directions of attention from
loved ones. These were considered in some detail in
The Supreme Adventure.[141] They are observed to occur
"at the very moment of transition," "just before the
end," and are recognized as "the immediate precursors
of death." There is no recorded case in which a dying
person claimed to see a "living" friend whom he er-
roneously thought to be dead—yet there are many instances in which dying people "saw" friends whom they
supposed to be "living" but who were, in fact, dead.
They say, "You didn't tell me that 'X' had died. Why
didn't you tell me?" Dr. Karl Osis,[142] Director of Re-

search, Parapsychology Foundation, Inc., New York, in *Deathbed Observations by Physicians and Nurses,* stated, "As a rule, the dying see visions with clear consciousness—they are not in a morbid or delirious state. Healthy persons hallucinate predominantly the living; terminal (dying) persons hallucinate predominantly the dead. . . . These are findings of major importance."

5. The direction of the attention of the dead toward (chiefly) loved ones whom they left on earth (this in addition to those who appear as deathbed visions) is another category in these phenomena. Many parents *"return" to try to help* the children left behind (as in the Jupp case, Gurney,[143] *Phantasms of the Living,* Holborn);[144] husbands "return" to comfort widows (e.g., the Samuel Bull case);[145] daughters "return" to prepare their mothers for their impending transition (e.g., the "red scratch" case);[146] employees "return" to vindicate their character (e.g., Robert Mackenzie);[147] fathers "return" to prevent injustices in relation to their wills (e.g., James Chaffin),[148] etc.

6. Another, surely significant, category includes those who "return" from "beyond" to appear to, or communicate with, those of the "living" with whom they made death-compacts during their earth lives. This category is related to that in which a living person makes up his mind, prior to going to sleep, to appear to a friend, noted above. Numerous death-compacts are eventually fulfilled: The attention of the contractor is successfully directed toward his friend after he has "passed on." Myers[149] pointed out that Gurney, struck by the number of successful death-compacts, concluded that they have "a certain efficiency."

It is evident that the "doubles," once released from the body, whether temporarily or permanently, are practically independent of physical space: They move instantly and automatically to a desired place. This is another of the many facts that indicate that most of the "doubles" of human beings are not, as many psychiatrists consider, mere mental images; since these seem to be the only "mental images" which (a) move to a desired place or person and (b) are, on some occasions, actually seen there by other persons.

The level of consciousness permitted by these (simple) "doubles." This was not "subnormal" or dreamy in any of these cases. There was no dual consciousness—such as occurs in cases in which the "doubles" included a significant portion of the vehicle of vitality. Consciousness characteristically included "super-normal" elements, such as telepathy (e.g., Mrs. Garrett, Mrs. Roberts, Mockler, Swedenborg), clairvoyance (e.g., Dr. Staver, Mrs. Garret, Miss Okeden, Dr. Alice Gilbert, Mrs. Vlasek, McCormack, R. J. Foy), and foreknowledge (e.g., Ronald Edwin).

Consciousness tended to be intense. Case No. 42 said, "I had been out of my body with my full personality, living and intensely aware—a real and very intense experience." Funk described "freedom and clearness of mental vision," Miss Addison's consciousness was "intensified," A. J. Mills was "never more clear-minded," Mrs. Roberts's consciousness "expanded."

(On our hypothesis, these are the normal levels of consciousness when we are free from the physical body, utilizing the unenshrouded Soul Body.)

The penultimate position of the returning "double."

Just as several people said their "doubles," immediately after quitting their bodies, were horizontal and above them, so several said that their returning "doubles" were horizontal, above their bodies. This was described by Ostby, Mrs. C. H. Smith, Dennis (two feet above), Mrs. Hibberd, and Miss Douglas. Mrs. Tolkein's "double" was "above her body." The rest, i.e., the majority, gave no such descriptions.

The repercussions and shock felt when the "double" reentered the body. In all these cases any rapid return, with shock, was due not to noises or other physical causes, but always to emotions felt by the person who was out of his body. This emotion was fear with Mrs. Sheridan, Varley, Sculthorpe, Mrs. Collins, A. J. Mills, Miss Griggs, Carrington's friends, Mrs. Burles, and Mrs. Mytton-Hall. With Lind, it was annoyance.

(On our hypothesis, all the facts are readily explained as due to "doubles" which were objective in nature—not mental images or "archetypes" in the "unconscious." They consisted of the "super-physical" Soul Body only. There are doubtless all gradations between these cases and [a] those of people who were slightly mediumistic and [b] those of people who were more or less exhausted or ill.)

GROUP IB.
"SEMI-PHYSICAL"
(*Vehicle of Vitality*)
"DOUBLES"

Facts:

1. In these cases also (Nos. 405, 413, 421, 431, 440, 442, 444, 457, 458—9 cases) there was a single stage in the formation (and in the disappearance) of the "doubles."
2. These "doubles" were never seen by the person who released them, but always by others, often by several others.
3. The persons concerned were probably of a mediumistic bodily constitution, i.e., with a somewhat loose "semi-physical" vehicle of vitality.
4. The state of health was probably only moderate—they were in a dreamy, preoccupied, slightly dissociated condition, with the attention directed toward some person or place that was distant from the physical body.
5. The "doubles" were not luminous, subtle, or tenuous; on the contrary, they were so apparently solid and lifelike as to be mistaken for physical bodies.
6. These "doubles" were not used as instruments of consciousness by the persons concerned.

Hypotheses:

Part of the "semi-physical" vehicle of vitality was released from the body: It was the "ghost" of a living man; it automatically obeyed the direction of the person's attention and was seen, by others, at some distance from the physical counterpart. Since the vehicle of vitality acts as a "bridge" between the Soul Body and the physical body but is not, by itself, an instrument of consciousness, this "double" could not be used for making observations. (A "double" must either consist of [Group I A] or include [Groups III and IV] the Soul Body, man's primary instrument of consciousness, if it is to be used to make observations.) Examples of cases of this type were not given in *The Study and Practice of Astral Projection,* 1961, or *More Astral Projections,* 1964. They are here given in Appendix II.

THIRD PART

Discussion

DISCUSSION

I. *Phenomena of the Release of "Doubles"*

Two of our groups consist of people who differ so far as their total bodily constitution is concerned: The presumed nonmediums who comprise Group I A, Second Part (and whose released "doubles" are interpreted as consisting of the "super-physical" Soul Body only) did not report observing such substances as "mist," "fog," "vapor," and "clouds" leave their bodies to form part of their "doubles." On the other hand, the known mediumistic people mentioned in the First Part commonly make such an observation. The latter saw (via the Soul Body) part of the "semi-physical" vehicle of vitality. Their "doubles" were, at least at first, composite.

There do not seem to be any significant differences, as regards our various groups, with respect either to the review of the past life or the "blackout." The latter might, of course, be expected, but the review is a noteworthy experience. In *The Supreme Adventure*[150] we

cited many "communicators" who have stated that they
underwent that experience in the early stages of transition—when they left the body permanently—and[151]
mentioned that many people who had left their bodies
temporarily, including those who were "sick unto death"
(and yet recovered), others who fell from great heights,
and still others who were nearly drowned, all described
having had the review of the past life.

We also indicated the probable cause of the experience.[152]

Since then we have found numerous further cases. For
example, Hudson Tuttle[153] mentioned an American who,
overtaken by a blizzard, was almost frozen to death and
who afterward said, "After the cold came a feeling of
comfort [since his "double" was out of his body], and
flashing pictures of events in his past. Then he began to
see friends who were long since dead. It was at this point
he was aroused [his "double" reentered his body] and
he felt angry . . . [was reluctant to leave "the next world"
and, by reentering his body, return to this world]." Tuttle also cited John Lamont, an Englishman of some note
who, when almost drowning, "experienced a strong illumination of spiritual powers [= an expansion of con-
sciousness] and a rapid review, like a panorama, of all
his past experiences." Moreover, he described having
had "a sort of double consciousness" [= our "dual consciousness" which occurs when the released "double" is
composite and near the body].

II. *The Environments Contacted*

Correlated with the fact that the members of Group I A (Soul Bodies) did not report observing "mist" leaving their bodies to form part of their "doubles" is the fact that none of them reported contacting the "misty," dim conditions that correspond to the vehicle of vitality (or "Hades" conditions). On the other hand, "mist" and "Hades" conditions were universally described by mediumistic people (First Part).

III. *The Initial Position of the Released "Doubles"*

People who claimed to leave their bodies temporarily all said that their "doubles" were above their bodies, and a number said that they were at first in a horizontal position, and not far above. The latter statement is corroborated by the testimony of Dr. R. B. Hout. He saw the permanently released "double" of his aunt—and it was in a horizontal position, above her body.

IV. *The Movements of the Released "Doubles"*

Whereas mediumistic people (whose "doubles" included a significant portion of the "semi-physical" vehicle of vitality) observed that, so long as they were near their bodies, they made movements that were identical with those of the physical counterpart—i.e., they were body-bound—the members of Group I A (whose "doubles" included no significant content of such substance) made no such observation.

v. *Effects of the Physical Senses on the "Doubles"*

Similarly, whereas mediumistically constituted people found that, when their "doubles" were near their bodies, they were affected by physical impacts; members of Group I A (Soul Bodies) made no such observations.

vi. *The Two-Stage Releases (and Two-Stage Returns) of Certain "Doubles"*

(involving [a] the first "death," followed by a "Hades" period, then [b] the second "death," followed by a "Paradise" period, and these, in certain cases, by [c] the reverse of the second "death," followed by a "Hades" period, then [d] the reverse of the first death [i.e., return to the physical body and earth conditions]). These facts are explicable on the objective body hypothesis, but are inexplicable on the subjective-mental image or "archetype" hypothesis. *In the entire history of psychology no one has described either mental images or "archetypes" that appear, and disappear, in two stages!*

The descriptions of out-of-the-body experiences, concerning (a) the first death (quitting or shedding the physical body), (b) the second "death" (the shedding of the vehicle of vitality from a composite "double") and concerning the return to the body, (c) the reassociation of the Soul Body with the vehicle of vitality (i.e., the reverse of the second "death"), followed by (d) the reassociation of the now composite "double" with the body (i.e., the reverse of the first death) are obviously concordant. Moreover, the facts are readily explained on the objective body hypothesis (where the vehicle of vitality and the corresponding environment, "Hades," often suggest "fog," "mist," "cloud," "vapor," even "water"). They are inexplicable on either of the subjective hypotheses.

After the first "blackout" (the first death), caused by the "double" separating from the body, we note that, in our intermediate (indefinite) cases (Appendix I) "mist" (which, on our hypothesis, represents part of the vehicle of vitality) was described by both Mrs. Veitch and Mrs. Mills as "cloud," by both Dr. Kirkland and Dr. Wiltse as "smoke," by Kirkland, Aridaeus, Mrs. Spaulding, Dr. Enid Smith, and Sir A. Ogston as "water." Mrs. Edwards described "mist" during the first stage of the release of her "double"; while during the second stage "cloud" was described by Yram, "fog" by Fox, and "water" by both Durman and Serrano. Among mediumistic people, "mist," "vapor" or "foam" was reported by "Reine," "clouds" by Muldoon, Cayce, Brown, and Hives, and "water" by Brown, Collier, and Mrs. Springer during the first stage of release; while during the first stage of return to the body Mrs. Cripps, Hives, and Mrs. Piper described "mist" and Mrs. Piper and

Professor Whiteman described "water." The vehicle of vitality is indicated in each case. Although not all mediumistic people who had out-of-the-body experiences described seeing such phenomena as "fog," "steam," or "water," this is not surprising: The ectoplasm (from the vehicle of vitality of a "physical" medium), at first invisible, often condenses and may be seen, photographed, and touched. Similarly, water-vapor which is at a very high temperature is invisible; lower the temperature and it condenses to form water: There is one physical substance in various stages of condensation.

The phenomena which clearly represent the vehicle of vitality were also compared to "gauzy" garments. In describing his second "death," Dr. Kirkland (Appendix II—intermediate cases) said, "My draperies [vehicle of vitality] clogged my feet and I [Soul Body] could scarcely crawl"; while Mrs. Dowell passed through "a veil of mist." With regard to Group III, in the first stage of the release of his "double," Badenhorst, the African native, described "a nebulous substance," while Mrs. Spaulding, in the second, spoke of "a seemingly gauze curtain." Among mediumistic people, Nancy Price, in the first stage of the release, described "a web," and in the second Mrs. Piper compared the feature to "a delicate blue drapery" and also to "a dark veil—a long robelike black thing." Lind spoke of "what seemed to be a child's dress."

In the first stage of her return to the body, Mrs. Piper described "a silk robe" which, she said, "swirled" over her [Soul Body's] head. Our interpretation of these descriptions (of *their own* vehicles of vitality) receives strong support from the accounts of people who saw the vehicle of vitality *of others*. For example, Dennis Bardens[154] recounted the experience of C. G. Barrie which included a phrase that is reminiscent of the "draperies," the "veil," the "robe," the "curtain," the "child's dress," the "nebulous substance," cited above. When passing a house, Bardens saw "what looked like a piece of diaphanous material." It passed through a closed window and "disappeared upwards." He learned later that a child had died at that moment in that house: He had seen —with his physical eyes—its "double" while it included the vehicle of vitality.

Relative dimness is commonly described in the environment ("Hades") that corresponds to the vehicle of vitality. Before the second "death," Dr. Kirkland said that all was "grey"; Percy Cole entered "a gloomy tunnel." Describing the second stage in the release of the "double," Helen Brooks spoke of "semi-darkness," Yram of "greyness," and Miss Horngate of "blackness." Turning to definitely mediumistic people, describing the first stage of release, Lane said that the light was "subdued," while Professor Whiteman stated it was "dark"; but in the second stage (after the second "death") all that was changed. Mme. d'Espérance said, "The light became intense." Hives entered "bright light." Mrs. Piper observed, "The whole earth was aglow," and, "Everything looked so bright." They had left "Hades" and entered "Paradise." Conversely, when Whiteman was returning to his body, he again entered "darkness."

"Wind" was mentioned only by those who were definitely of the mediumistic bodily constitution (First Part), and only in relation to the first stage in the release of the "double" and the first stage in its return:

Thus Miss Johnson described "cold air" and "a 'spirit-of-the-wind' sensation" on release, and Hives a "rushing wind" on both release and return.

Sounds (that seemed to accompany the release of the "double" from the body) were restricted to the same two processes. As her "double" left her body Nancy Price heard a sound "like tearing silk" and Mme. Bois-sou "a sort of silky rustle"; while, as the "double" began to reenter the body, Professor Whiteman heard a sound like "rushing water" and Mme. Boissou "the same gentle rustle" as when she left her body. Strange super-normal "winds" and sounds—especially sounds like those of "water"—are among ectoplasmic phenomena of psychical research, ectoplasm being derived from the vehicle of vitality. The descriptions of "winds" and sounds of "water" and similar sounds accord with our hypothesis that, at this stage in their development, these "doubles" included a significant portion of the vehicle of vitality.

The feelings described by these mediumistically constituted people who had out-of-the-body experiences were significantly concordant under the diverse conditions; and they agree with those of "physical" mediums who have extruded ectoplasm from the vehicle of vitality. Among the intermediate cases, Kirkland, when passing through the second "death," felt "cold." Yram found the "atmosphere" to be "irksome to bear"—he felt "oppression" and had "a general malaise." Among the definitely mediumistic people, Professor Whiteman, when passing through the first death, felt "confused." Lane felt "a gentle swish" pass from his feet to his head, and his "double" was then free. Mme. d'Espérance felt "stifled" and "cramped," and "cold." The second "death" (the process of shedding the vehicle of vitality from the hitherto composite "double") gave Mme. d'Espérance "a sense of motion," Miss Johnson "a rushing sensation" (after which bright and happy "Paradise" conditions were entered in the now unenshrouded Soul Body). Professor Whiteman then contacted "utter reality": He said, "I have never been awake before!" *But when he began to return to his body—and first to reassociate with his vehicle of vitality, passing through the reverse of the second "death" and once more briefly contacting "Hades" conditions—Whiteman's feelings included "fear" (which, as we have seen, is often experienced in that region), doubtless partly because it is abnormal to man and partly because of "hinderers."*

The "Hades" environment which was contacted so long as the "double" included part of the vehicle of vitality was observed to include both antagonistic and wraithlike beings; hence, of course, Whiteman's fears. Among our intermediate cases (Appendix I) Aridaeus saw the latter "drifting aimlessly" and Percy Cole was passed by "a stream of shadows." Edwin also saw "shadowy people." These may have been discarnate souls who, having lived exceptionally aimless earth lives, had become mere "shadows" of human beings. Some may have been "astral shells," such as clairvoyants (including the Reverend William Stainton Moses) observed in graveyards. In other words, they may have been vehicles of vitality which had been discarded at the second "death" and which, we are told by Dr. Rudolf Steiner, C. W. Leadbeater, and others, decay *pari passu* with the physical body. Yram encountered active "hinderers" with "grinning faces." Hives saw "drifting wraiths" both just after leaving his body (while his "double" was composite) and again just before reentering it (that is, after he, like Professor Whiteman, had just passed through *the reverse of the second "death"* and his "double" was again composite).

The distance between the released "double" and the vacated body was also described, by several independent deponents, in significant terms. Muldoon's "double" was obliged to move at least fifteen feet from his body in order to get rid of the vehicle of vitality and to be free of its pull (the distance was not fixed but varied with his health). D'nartsa's distance was three to four feet, and Dr. Simon's was six feet. These distances, described by projectors as applying to their own temporarily released (composite) "doubles" are, of course, concordant with the relatively short distances described by the numerous people who have observed the permanently released (composite) "doubles" of the dying—these also were only a few feet. In both cases, since the "doubles" included a significant amount of the "semi-physical" vehicle of vitality, they were "body-bound."

The series of experiences described above, whether including a reverse of the second "death" or not, was followed by a "blackout" in consciousness as the "double" reengaged with the body. This, of course, was the reverse of the first death—which began with a "blackout." As Hives said, the phenomena which he observed just after he left his body were again encountered just before he reentered it (after the reverse of the second "death"; others gave descriptions of this state of affairs but did not make the generalization).

Those "doubles" with which were associated descriptions of "fog," "water," "dimness," darkness, rustling sounds, the sound of "water," fear, confusion, sensations of being stifled or oppressed, the sight of floating wraiths and mocking "hinderers"—that is, those of definitely mediumistic people (First Part)—were all interpreted, on other grounds, as including a significant amount of the vehicle of vitality. On the other hand, those "doubles" that were not associated with "fog" (Group I A) show no evidence of including that substance; they evidently consisted of the Soul Body only.

Practically all the cases mentioned above were moderns. Anna Maria Roos[155] referred to a work of the second century that contained references to corresponding experiences in trance states ("somnambulism"). The philosopher Apuleius went to be initiated into the Mysteries of Isis, the ancient Egyptian deity. The preparations included fasting (a procedure which tends to cause a partial release of the vehicle of vitality). Fasting tends to increase the intake of cosmic vitality, and consequently to release the Soul Body, since the vehicle of vitality is the "bridge" between the two bodies. The initiates, whether of the mediumistic or nonmediumistic type, thus tended to release a "double" that was composite— part of the vehicle of vitality, corresponding to the "Hades" belt of the earth, accompanied by the Soul Body, corresponding to the "Paradise" belt of the earth.

On returning to his body, and therefore to what we necessarily regard as "normal" consciousness, the initiate said, "Approaching the borderland of death, I stepped over the threshold [the "double" quitting the body] and

was conducted through the 'elements.' Although it was
midnight [on earth], the light was brilliant. I stepped
into the presence of the 'gods' [= saw spirits of the dead]
of the underworld ["Hades"] and the 'gods' [spirits of
the dead] of the upper world ["Paradise"]."

Miss Roos found that the descriptions of "somnambulists" in Europe, i.e., people who were in mesmeric
trance (also releasing a "double" that was composite),
could be summed up as follows: *First, during the actual
'passing over,' there is a region of darkness through
which one must pass [= the "blackout" as the "double"
separates from the body] then a roaring 'river' which
must be crossed, i.e., the element of 'water' [= the
"Hades" belt or aura of the earth, corresponding to the
vehicle of vitality which enshrouds the released Soul
Body], then [after the second "death," the shedding of
the vehicle of vitality from the composite "double"] a
brilliant light [of the subtle "Paradise" belt or aura of
the earth], i.e., the element of 'fire' eventually circles the
Soul [since it is now unenshrouded]: Through the air
[the super-terrestrial "Paradise" aura of the earth] they
float, leaving the earth beneath their feet [the Soul Body,
being "super-physical" in nature, defying gravity]." Our
study shows that this succession of events and
experiences, described eighteen centuries ago in Egypt
by carefully selected Initiates of the Mysteries, and
approximately a century ago in France, England, etc.,
by people who underwent mesmeric trance, were also
described in recent years by people all over the world
who were neither Initiates nor in a condition of mes-*

meric trance. Four matters applied to all: (a) "Doubles" left physical bodies; (b) they rose above their bodies; (c) they first contacted "Hades" conditions; and (d) they then contacted "Paradise" conditions.

"Thus," pointed out Miss Roos, "the aim of the Mysteries was a state of trance in which the aspirant was transported into another world [first into the dim "Hades" and later the bright "Paradise"—with the second "death," the crossing of "water" in between]." It was chiefly because some of these visitors to "the next world" were of low moral and spiritual development and consequently did not get past the dim and fearful "Hades" region, with its wraiths and possible "hinderers," that psychic matters have had such a bad "press" down the years. Those who are not morally and spiritually "ready" should avoid making such attempts. In fact, we do not advocate deliberate out-of-the-body experiences at all. What comes naturally is in a different category.

Miss Roos concluded, "We understand why the initiated affirm their certainty of a life after death. All who have had any experience of deep somnambulism [= "super-normal" consciousness of, mesmeric trance] are certain that what they saw was real and no dream or vision [compare Professor Whiteman, who, in his out-of-the-body experiences, contacted "utter reality"]."

E. G. Collinge[156] similarly said that the first object of initiation by the Priests of Osiris (the husband of Isis) was the release of the "double" (in this case by hypnosis and ceremonies) giving eventual consciousness of "Paradise" conditions and thus furnishing "proof, instead of blind faith, of survival." But this assurance is confined, of course, to the initiates: It cannot be transmitted to noninitiates: "If you say you have a revelation," said Benjamin Whichcote, "I must have a revelation too, before I can believe you." On the other hand, the experiences described by ancient initiates and by people who were in deep mesmeric trance—first of "Hades" with its possible "hinderers' and later of "Paradise" with its helpers—are identical with those described by many hundreds of moderns who are of the mediumistic bodily constitution. This is surely significant.

VII. *The "Silver Cord"-Extension*

It will be remembered that Professor C. J. Ducasse pointed out that, if astral projectors' descriptions of a "silver cord" which united the "double" to the body should prove to be the actual state of affairs, then these "doubles" would not—as most psychiatrists and medical men suppose—be mental images of physical bodies but "sights . . . of something objectively present at the place where they are perceived." We venture to suggest that the psychiatrists and medical men, before declaring their views, failed to assemble and analyze the facts. There is good evidence that numerous people had a "silver cord" which united their temporarily released "doubles" to their temporarily vacated bodies.

A. PEOPLE WHO DID NOT SEE, BUT FELT, THE PRESENCE OF THEIR ''SILVER CORDS''

In our Group II, Frances Gail felt that she was "still tied" to her body. The African native said he was "still attached" to his: "A strange power," namely, its strong elasticity, "pulled him back." Rosamund Lehmann first felt "a violent tugging" at the solar plexus and then found that her "double" was being "forcibly ejected." Alain Bain also had a sensation at the solar plexus. Sir A. Ogston, who nearly died, stated, "My mental self used regularly to leave my body always carrying something black and soft, I did not know what, in my left hand." In our Group III, Mrs. Leonard felt the presence of her "cord" but apparently never actually saw it. Durman's "double" was forced back to his body by "a strong elastic force." Mrs. Edwards felt "a sharp tug" and was back in her body.

B. PEOPLE WHO SAW AND DESCRIBED THEIR OWN ''SILVER CORDS''

1. *Simple terms*

(a) *A "cord"*—In Group I A, Mrs. Argles, Mrs. May, Mrs. Haynes, Ibbetson (cord to head), Keane ("cord, smoky, silver color and about a half to three-eighths of an inch thick"), Goddard ("a band like a cord—to the head), Mrs. Helm ("a slight cord"), Dr. Alice Gilbert ("a cloudy-looking cord"), the Tibetans ("an almost impalpable cord"), Mrs. Williams ("a shining white cord" —attached to the head) and Mrs. "Mansergh" ("a glistening cord"). Among our intermediate cases, Weatherhead's friend ("something in the nature of a cord"), Gaythorpe, "Prothero," Wiltse ("a small cord like a spider's web"), Turvey ("This cord is very like a spider's cord. It is silver tinged with heliotrope and it extends and contracts as does an elastic cord. The cord appears whenever the 'I' leaves the 'me.' "), Mrs. Webb ("a queer cord"), and Yram ("a kind of cord").

(b) *A "chain"*—In Group I A, Wirt described "a silver cord or chain."

(c) *A "strand"*—In Group I A, the Tibetans described "a strand."

(d) *A "tape" or "band"*—Among intermediate cases, Dr. Matthiessen's *eleven-year-old child* ("a band or cord"), Karreman (*a non-English-speaking African, describing what he saw as a child of nine to ten years*—"a tape"—see also his description given below, of the pulsation of vitality in his "cord"), Gerhardi, the English writer ("an uncanny tape of light, like the umbilical cord"—see also his description given below, of its vital function), Badenhorst (another African) "a band"—see also his description, given below, of its pulsating with vitality.

(e) *An "arm"*—This term was used by Mr. Bytheway (intermediate).

(f) *A "thread"*—Intermediates include Stuart-Young ("the thread that holds me to life"), the man with a weak heart ("a shadowy thread" which was joined to the head of his body—he also called it "an ethereal thread"), Fox ("a shining silver thread"), Yram ("invisible threads"), Huntley ("a feeble thread"), the mediumistic "Kenwood" ("a long silver thread"—he thought, "I must not break that cord!" It got very short and his "double" began to enter his body.).

(g) *A "string"*—In Group I A both Mrs. Doan and Mrs. "T. D." ("a smoky string"), Mrs. Folson (*when a child of five to six years*—"a sort of lustrous 'kite-string,' as I called it in my mind").

(h) *A "connection"*—Yram (intermediate).

(i) *A "ribbon"*—Group I A, Mrs. Matile ("greasy-like ribbon"), Moss ("a long ribbon"—to the head). Intermediate case: Mrs. Wahl (*an African*—"a silver ribbon about two inches wide").

(j) *A "pipeline"*—Group I A, Mrs. Hutchinson ("a kind of pipeline"—which guided her released "double" back to her vacated body).

(k) *A "neck"*—Intermediate case: the Dr. Schultz case ("like a long neck").

2. *Descriptive terms*

(a) *"A silver cord"*—(Compare Ecclesiastes xii, 6— "Or ever the silver cord be loosed . . . then shall the dust return to the earth as it was and the Spirit shall return unto God Who gave it.") Group I A—Lester Wirt ("a silver cord or chain"). Intermediate cases: Findlay's acquaintance, the soldier ("a slender cord of silvery appearance"—he, much like Mrs. Hutchinson, cited above [No. 10] described his return to the body as follows: "I came down that silver cord and returned to my old body"). Mediumistic people—Muldoon, Evan Powell, and Mrs. Cripps ("the silver cord").

(b) *"A silvery cord"*—Group I A, Mrs. Webb.

(c) *A "beam," "shaft," or "coil" of light*—Intermediate cases: An anonymous lady was "connected to her body by something that looked like a beam of light." Gerhardi, "a coil of light—like a luminous garden hose, resembling the broad ray of dusty light at the back of a dark cinema projecting on to the screen in front." Gerhardi also compared what he saw to "a lighted cord." Mrs. Herrick ("a long cord or streamer of light"), Mrs. Clayton ("a silver thread of light"), *McCreery's child informant ("a sunbeam"—down which, much like Mrs. Hutchinson and the soldier just cited, she "slid" back to her body*). Mediumistic cases: Sullivan saw "what looked like a thin ray of golden light"—it was joined to his solar plexus.

The son of P. J. Hitchcock[157] got out of bed during the night and went along a passage. He "became conscious that something was amiss" (i.e., that he was out of his body in the released "double"). He *looked back* and saw what appeared to be *a thin cord of light* going back from himself ("double") into his bedroom. Anxiously, he turned and followed the "cord" back and was startled to see himself (physical body) lying asleep. He did not know how he got back into his body.

3. *The composition and the attachment of the "cord."*

A few who observed their own "silver cords" noted that they actually consisted of a number of "threads," and that these spread out at the point of attachment. Mrs. Folson, when a child "younger than five or six," made this observation: There were "many fine threads which joined to make a single strand that floated rather like a cobweb" which was attached to her body. She was somehow aware that if she broke this "string" she "couldn't get back" (i.e., her body would die for lack of the vitality it transmitted).

4. *Vitality seen to be pulsating in the "cord."*

It is presumably vitality that gives the "cord" its silvery appearance (so that if the vitality is very high the "cord" may be very bright but if, as with the pseudo-dead Sir A. Ogston, it is very low, the "cord" may be "black" while, intermediate between these extremes there are "cloudy-looking cords," as with Dr. Gilbert). *The pulsation of vitality is described only in connection with composite "doubles."*

Karreman, the African who described an out-of-the-body experience that had occurred to him when nine to ten years of age, said that his "cord" was pulsating: Every time it pulsated, it had "a phosphorescent light." William Gerhardi, the eminent English literary man, made the same observation: As already said, he described his "cord" as "an uncanny tape of light like the umbilical cord"—and he added "by means of which the body on the bed was kept breathing." Among intermediate cases, Badenhorst described a "band" which pulsated with vitality—it bore "tiny spots of brilliance" that resembled diamonds. Mrs. Porter also observed this phenomenon. Mrs. Gwen Cripps observed that her "cord" pulsated with "life."

5. *The conditions under which these people saw their own "cords."*

Some would-be skeptics have suggested that narratives of out-of-the-body experiences were either mere dreams or deliberate inventions, but neither they nor the narrators realized that a number of highly significant matters, unforeseen by either the deponents or their detractors, are revealed by careful studies of the testimonies.

The "cord" forms, as Turvey observed, when the "double" leaves the body. He also noted that it is reabsorbed when the "double" reenters the body. Many others made the latter observation, stating it in convincing terms. Thus, Crabbe's soldier whose "double" was above his body, said, "I came down that silver cord and returned to the old body"; while Mrs. Hutchinson said, "I found a kind of pipeline which guided me back to my body." Mrs. Gaythorpe returned "down a long steep 'road'" (? "the cord"); and Mrs. Piper stated, "I came in on a cord, a silver cord."

We note that, if the released "double" was described as having left the body and having risen above it, the "cord" was described as seen when the person concerned *looked down.* This was the case with the Reverend L. J. Bertrand, Oliver Fox, Mrs. Boorman ("I saw my physical body lying on the bed. I also noticed a silver light between me and my body"), Mrs. "Prothero," Mrs. Argles ("looking down on my body. . . . There was a cord connecting me to the body. . . ."). On the other hand, if the "double" was described as having erected and as being in the course of moving forward, away from the body, the "cord" was described by those who "turned round," as with Hitchcock's son, cited above. It was not so described by those who did not. Thus, Dr. Wiltse said, "Looking back, I saw a small cord like a spider's web"; while Muldoon stated, "I managed to turn round —there was another 'me' lying quietly on the bed. My two identical bodies were joined by means of an elastic-like cable." William Gerhardi used this fact to prove to himself the reality of his out-of-the-body experience. He asked himself, "How do I know that I am not dreaming this?" and answered, "Look for the lighted cord behind you!" He looked, saw it, and was satisfied. Later Gerhardi said, "I wonder whether I may not have died unawares? I . . . turned round. But the silver cord, faint and thin, was still there." Wirt said, "I float out of, and away from my fleshly form. . . . I now look back and see my body . . . and further I see the silver cord or chain connecting my Spiritual [Astral or Soul] Body with the earthly." Margaret Newby knew that she had failed to see her "cord" because she had failed to look down from her released "double" toward her body. These cases are chiefly British and American. Here is one from Norway: Ingeborg, the daughter of Judge Dahl, out of her body, observed a "cord" and said, "It is following me." Several astral projectors, including Mrs. "Mansergh," Mrs. Matile, and Yram, similarly described their "cords" as "trailing" behind their forward-moving "doubles."

C. PEOPLE WHO SAW AND DESCRIBED THE ''SILVER CORDS'' OF OTHERS

1. *The "cord" of a living person (who was ill)*

"A band"—the friend of the lady journalist who had a serious nervous breakdown saw "bands of light" which streamed from the released "double" to the vacated body.

2. *The "cords" of living persons (who were anesthetized)*

"A shaft"—Dr. R. B. Hout saw three patients whose "doubles" had been ejected from their bodies by anesthetics: Each "double" was joined to its physical body by "a silvery shaft of light."

3. *The "cords" of the dying*

"A cord"—J. C. Street, who saw "vapor" leave a dying body and gradually assume the form of the person concerned, observed that it was at first "about a foot" above the body to which it was attached by "a slender cord." This snapped. Mr. "G" (whose testimony was published by the Society for Psychical Research)[158] similarly saw "clouds" when his wife died; and these gradually became a replica, or "double," which was in a horizontal position and was attached to her body by "a cord." The latter was "suddenly severed." Dr. Burgess, an expert in nervous and mental diseases, who was also present at this "passing," wrote: "From my observations, I can most

positively put aside a temporary acute state of hallucinatory insanity during the time of the vision just recorded. . . . I knew Mr. 'G' well. I had occasion to know that he had not read anything in the occult line." Miss F. E. Porter, present at the "passing" of a man, saw "the silver cord": It pulsated with vitality. She observed, "It appeared to be vibrating as though a light were flashing up and down." Gordon Turner[159] also saw "a silver cord" at a deathbed.

Dr. R. B. Hout[160] saw his aunt release her "double" permanently. Hout said, "My attention was called . . . to something immediately above the physical body, suspended in the atmosphere about two feet above the bed. At first I could distinguish nothing more than a vague outline of a hazy, foglike substance. There seemed to be only a mist held suspended, motionless. But, as I looked, very gradually there grew into my sight a denser, more solid, condensation of this inexplicable vapor. Then I was astonished to see definite outlines presenting themselves, and soon I saw this foglike substance was assuming a human form.

"Soon I knew that the body I was seeing resembled that of the physical body of my aunt [it was her "double"]. . . . The astral body hung suspended horizontally a few feet above the physical counterpart. . . . I continued to watch and . . . the Spirit Body now seemed complete to my sight. I saw the features plainly. They were very similar to the physical face, except that a glow of peace and vigor was expressed instead of age and pain. The eyes were closed as though in tranquil sleep, and a luminosity seemed to radiate from the Spirit Body.

"As I watched the suspended Spirit Body, my atten-

tion was called, again intuitively, to a silverlike substance that was streaming from the head of the physical
body to the head of the spirit 'double.' Then I saw the
connection-cord between the two bodies. As I watched,
the thought, 'The silver cord!' kept running through my
mind. I knew, for the first time, the meaning of it. This
'silver cord' was the connecting-link between the physical and the spirit bodies, even as the umbilical cord
unites the child to its mother. . . ." [Compare the cogi-
tations of Peter M. Urquhart, Case No. 170, when he
saw his own "silver cord" during a temporary out-of-the-
body experience. Again, when the Reverend Dr. Staver,
whose testimony is cited below, saw "a wisp of connection which remained for some little time" joining his
newly dead father to the latter's newly released "double,"
he said, "It reminded me of the oft-mentioned 'silver
cord.' "]

Hout continued, "The cord was attached to each of
the bodies at the occipital protuberance immediately at
the base of the skull. Just where it met the physical body
it spread out, fanlike, and numerous little strands separated and attached separately to the skull base. But other
than at the attachments, the cord was round, being perhaps about an inch in diameter. The colour was a translucent luminous silver radiance. The cord seemed alive
with vibrant energy. I could see the pulsations of light
stream along the course of it, from the direction of the
physical body to the spirit 'double.' With each pulsation
the spirit body became more alive and denser, whereas
the physical body became quieter and more nearly lifeless. . . .

"By this time the features were very distinct. The life

was all in the astral body. . . . The pulsations of the cord had stopped. . . . I looked at the various strands of the cord as they spread out, fanlike, at the base of the skull. Each strand snapped . . . the final severance was at hand. A twin process of death and birth was about to ensue. . . . The last connecting strand of the silver cord snapped and the spirit body was free.

"The spirit body, which had been supine [horizontal] before, now rose. . . . The closed eyes opened and a smile broke from the radiant features. She gave a smile of farewell, then vanished from my sight.

"The above phenomenon was witnessed by me as an entirely objective reality. The spirit-forms I saw with the aid of my physical eye . . . [compare our observations made in the Introduction, and Richet's insistence that the preliminary "fog" seen leaving dying bodies was not imaginary but an objective phenomenon]." This medical man, Dr. Hout, had, indeed, witnessed not merely the process which to us mortals is death, but also that which is revealed to only a few fortunate eyes—the process of survival—"the twin process of death and birth."

The description of E. W. Oaten[161] when he observed the "passing" of a friend named Daisy is essentially similar. "I saw a faint, smokelike vapor rise from the body. It rose some few feet above the bed and stayed there. . . . It condensed and grew larger, supplied with a steady stream from the body, a stream of vapor some three inches in diameter. . . . Then gradually, definition began to come. It assumed the form of a roughly moulded dummy of the human form. . . .

"An umbilical cord united it with the physical body. I could see the flow of energy (pulsating) in the umbilical cord. Presently there was the exact duplicate of Daisy floating . . . in the air. It was connected to the body by the silver cord through which her life slowly escaped. Then the form began to heave and rock, like a balloon tearing at its moorings. The silver cord began to stretch. It grew thinner and thinner at the middle until at last it snapped and the floating form assumed an upright attitude. It was the living duplicate of the sleeping form on the bed. She turned to me and smiled. She was thanking me for the hours I had spent in trying to help her. . . . Then . . . she floated away."

M. H. Tester[162] described how he and his sister saw the "passing" of their father. Two hours before "the end" the body became comatose (i.e., it had been vacated by most of the vehicle of vitality, the "bridge" between it and the Soul Body). This is commonly the case—most people die in their "sleep." The account continues, "At that moment, before our eyes, the life force (= vehicle of vitality) started to go from him. His Spirit (= the now composite "double," consisting of both the Soul Body and the vehicle of vitality) left his body and drifted away, connected only by the 'silver cord.' Gradually the 'cord' lengthened as his Spirit moved further away: *It continued to pulse slowly. . . . Then the 'silver cord' stopped pulsing. . . .* It dissolved. . . . My father was 'dead.' "

Rose Harley[163] said, "Once, in a hospital ward, I saw a patient's 'spirit' leave the body. It rose like a white mist and stood upright at the foot of the bed. There was a silvery thread from the nape of its neck to the body. Then that snapped, and it was gone."

Writing from the United States of America, the Reverend Dr. R. J. Staver[164] told me how he was present at the "passing" of his father. He said, "The withdrawal was . . . from the top of the head. . . . There was a little mistlike wraith which rose rather slowly. . . . It had no human appearance at the time of withdrawal; that came a bit later. The whole proceeding took the best part of an hour, and for some time following the complete withdrawal, there was a wisp of connection between the physical body and that portion which had left it— it reminded me of the oft-mentioned 'silver cord.' "

From India, V. D. Rishi[165] wrote, "The outline body ["double"] starts emerging from the head in the form of a cloud of vapour. This condenses and gradually forms into a replica of the dying person. When the [new] body is completely formed, a process which usually takes from one to two hours, it stands erect over the prostrate body, yet connected by a 'cord' about two feet long, similar to the umbilical cord of earthly birth. The dying man's last gasp indicates the snapping of the 'cord' and the completion of the death process." (In rare instances, however, as with Stainton Moses's father, the "loosing" of the "cord" is somewhat delayed—there is still vitality in the body, even though return to it is impossible.)

H. A. and F. H. Curtiss[166] observed that, "The astral 'double' is attached to the physical body by an astral cord, something like an umbilical cord." They added, "This does not permit it to withdraw very far from the physical. . . ." (Note the distances cited: the Indian Rishi ["two feet"]; the Americans, Dr. Davis ["near the ceiling"—say four or five feet] and Dr. Hout ["a few feet]; the British women, Florence Marryat ["two to three feet"] and Mrs.

Taylor ["three feet"]; and the British men, J. C. Street ["a foot"], Oaten ["some few feet"], Hodgson ["just above"], and the Reverend Stainton Moses ["a quarter of a yard"]. We correlate this remarkably close proximity of the newly released "double" to the corpse—which contrasts with the absolute freedom of the newly released "doubles" that comprise our Group I A, interpreted as representing Soul Bodies only—with the hypothesis that death is due to the release from a dying body of the whole of the vehicle of vitality, as well as the Soul Body. The latter quits easily and rapidly, the former is completely released slowly and with difficulty: It never gets far from the body to which it really belongs.)

"Cords of light, like electricity"—Florence Marryat's description was similar to those of Dr. Hout and E. W. Oaten: "A cloud of smoke gathered above her head. It spread out and acquired the shape of the girl's body. It was suspended in the air two or three feet above the body. . . . When she lay back unconscious, *the Spirit above, which was still bound to her brain, heart and vitals by cords of light like electricity, became, as it were, a living Soul.* Then . . . she stood upright, the living presentment of the body which now stretched out in death. The spirits of her father and grandmother appeared. They ruptured with their hands the cords that bound her to her body. Rising between them, she vanished."

Leslie Curnow[167] published the description of Mrs. Watts, who observed, *"a delicate gleaming line or cord of light."*

Geoffrey Hodson[168] described the "double" of a dying man as floating "just above" his body and as *"joined to it by a stream of flowing forces which shine with a delicate silver light."* He stated, "When the 'silver cord' is seen to break, the man himself [in the "double"] rises as though released from some gravitational pull. . . . The signs of death appear in the body."

The Reverend William Stainton Moses[169] observed many "passings" and summarized what he had seen: "When you have finished with your fleshly form, your spirit body ("double") will rise out of it, an exact facsimile of it. First, the spirit form, which is unconscious at the time, commences to rise from the top of the head and slowly ascends. . . . Then the spirits who are there to receive the spirit body ["deliverers"] hold out their arms to support it, until the 'cord' . . . has 'passed.' *The 'cord' is usually about a quarter of a yard long."*

H. E. Hunt (*in litt.*) saw an old lady die. He said: "The almost wornout body . . . was apparently maintained by a thin white cord of light. . . . Three spirits bent over the dying woman and passed their hands over her form. . . . The last sign of movement left the body. . . . *The cord of light instantly disappeared."*

Mrs. Josephine Taylor (*in litt.*) told how she saw a child die: "I saw a mist above the little body. It took the shape of the body which lay on the bed. This was attached by *a very fine silver cord.* . . . The replica was about three feet above the body, then gradually tilted itself into an upright position. It then floated away."

Charles Moore[170] observed, "There slowly escapes from the outworn body a luminous cloud of fine substance. This rapidly becomes compact and takes the form of a solid ethereal body exactly like the old physical body from which it has arisen. . . . Natural decease is practically the same as falling asleep, but with no returning owing to *the severance of the psychic umbilical cord which unites the spirit with the body.*"

Dr. A. J. Davis[171] published detailed descriptions of "passings" a century ago. Like Leadbeater, Phoebe Payne, and other clairvoyants (as well as "communicators" such as Fr. Greber's in Germany and "Ambrose Pratt," Dr. Raynor C. Johnson's in Great Britain) he stated that the "spiritual," or Soul Body, is related to the physical body by means of "vital electricity"—and to the Spirit by "vital magnetism." The following account of a "passing" was published in *The Physician*, 1850.[172] "The head becomes enveloped in a fine, luminous atmosphere. I saw, in the atmosphere, the distinct outline of another head, then the development of the neck, the shoulders and the entire spiritual organisation ["double"]. The spirit ["double"] rose at right angles over the body. But, immediately previous to the final dissolution, I saw, playing energetically between the feet of the elevated spiritual body and the prostrate physical form, *a bright stream or current of vital electricity* [*the "silver cord"*]. This taught me that death is but a birth of the spirit from a lower into a higher state, that the correspondence between the birth of a child into this world and the birth of the spirit from a material body into a higher world is absolute and complete—even to *the umbilical cord, which was represented by the thread of vital electricity,* which for a few minutes connected the two organisms."

Here is another description by Dr. Davis:[173] "The feet become cold first. One sees right over the head what may be called a magnetic halo—an ethereal emanation, golden in appearance ["double"]. Now the body is cold up to the knees. . . . The emanation is more expanded . . . and attains a position near the ceiling. The person has ceased to breathe. The emanation ["double"] is elongated and fashioned in the outlines of the human form. It is connected [by the "silver cord"] beneath with the brain. The thinking faculties are rational, while nearly every part of the person is dead. The golden emanation ["double"] is connected with the brain by a very fine life-thread [the "silver cord"]. On the body of the emanation there appears something white and shining, like a human head; next comes a faint outline of the face; the neck and shoulders manifest, and then, in rapid succession, all parts of the new body. . . . *The fine life-thread continues attached to the old brain. The next thing is the withdrawal of this electrical principle. When the thread snaps the spiritual body is free.* The spirit-being is asleep; the eyes are closed . . . it speeds to the world of light ["Paradise"].

Another early case of this type is by Hudson Tuttle.[174] It should be noted that this man lived in a farmhouse remote from any town, and had access to few books. He stated, "I had attended school eleven months in all." His description of a "passing" is as follows: "Slowly the spiritual body withdrew from the extremities and concentrated in the brain. As it did so, a halo arose from the crown of the head and gradually increased. Soon it became clear and distinct, and I observed that it had the exact resemblance of the form it had left. Higher and higher it rose until the beautiful spirit stood before us and the body reclined below. *A light cord connected the two, which gradually diminished.*"

Estelle Roberts[175] described her husband's transition. "I saw his spirit leave the body. It emerged from his head and gradually moulded itself into an exact replica of his earth-body. *It remained suspended about a foot above his body, lying in the same position [i.e., horizontal], and attached to it by a cord to the head. Then the cord broke and the spirit-form floated away, passing through the wall.*"

A "connection"—Dr. D. P. Kayner[176] saw a fellow physician, a Dr. Cross, die: He observed "a vapor or mist" which left the chest and head and "gradually rose" until the "newly born man" stood up. He tried to express his thanks to Kayner (as did Dr. Hout's newly dead aunt, Oaten's friend, and others), and then the connection was severed. The process was completed.

A "thread"—As already said, Rose Harley, at a hospital, saw a patient's "double" leave his body and said, "There was a silvery thread from the nape of its neck to the body. Then that snapped and it was gone."

D. PREHISTORIC DESCRIPTIONS
OF THE ''SILVER CORD''
(TEMPORARY RELEASES OF
''DOUBLES'')

Professor M. Eliade[177] published an outstanding work on prehistoric shamans (priest-healers) who claimed to quit their bodies and ascend to bright "Paradise" conditions: He insisted that, behind the myths and symbols which were used by these pre-literate men in numerous countries, there lies the idea of achievement of communication between mortals on earth and "gods"—usually meaning discarnate human souls who were possible helpers and advisers. Moreover, according to the shamans, the ascent involved a "crossing" of the dim and danger- ous "Hades" belt with its possible "hinderers."

Eliade considers that such symbols as a "ladder," a "tree," a "vine," a "chain," or a "cord" were the "physi- cal means" of this ascent into "Paradise." We would point out that it was, of course, natural that when these prehistoric and illiterate men achieved the release of their "doubles" from their bodies and the ascent into "Para- dise" conditions—and saw their "silver cords"—they should, on return, describe the "cords" as means of ascent, by analogy with physical means of climbing above the earth. Professor Eliade did not realize that the released "double" is an objective body, and that the "cord," "chain," or other connection that appeared with its release was also objective—an extension, in fact, of both body and "double."

Professor Eliade gave the geographical distribution of the various terms used by the ancient shamans. The terms, when compared with those used by moderns who had out-of-the-body experiences (whether naturally, or due to falls, anesthetics, or impending dissolution), obvi- ously refer to "the silver cord."

A *"cord"*—Australia

A *"ribbon"* or a *"rainbow"*—(a) Asia, the Hawaiian Islands, Japan, Mesopotamia (b) Polynesia, Indonesia, Melanesia, Japan

A *"rope"*—North Africa, Tibet, Australia, Manchuria, India

A *"thread"*—a *"bridge"* that was *"as narrow as a hair"* —Africa, Central Asia

A *"stick"* or *"post"*—Hungary, Asia

A *"ladder"*—Greece, Tibet, Borneo, Sarawak, South America, Dutch Guiana

A *"tree"*—Asia

A *"vine"*—New Zealand

It will be evident that "the silver cord" mentioned by Ecclesiastes has been known to mankind from time immemorial—but its true significance is only now coming to be recognized.

E. PRIMITIVES' DESCRIPTIONS OF THE ''CORDS'' OF THE DYING

The natives of Tahiti, in the South Pacific, were unable to read or write (and consequently to obtain ideas at second-hand from Europeans).

F. THE ''SILVER CORDS'' OF MATERIALIZED FIGURES

Reference to the numerous photographs of materializations (by Schrenck Notzing[178]) will show that the released ectoplasmic figure, representing substance from the vehicle of vitality of the medium, is often joined to the body by a thin, spiderlike "silver cord." This feature was objective. These phantoms grade imperceptibly into the denser type of the "doubles" of astral projectors, namely, the composite "doubles," those of "physical" mediums. The inference concerning the nature of the "silver cord" is obvious. Both "doubles" and their "silver cords" vary greatly in density—and this may apply, as we have seen, to the "doubles" released under different conditions by one and the same person. Both Yram in France and Fox in England sometimes released an unusually dense "double" (and realized that it included part of the "semi-physical" "etheric double," or vehicle of vitality), whereas they usually released a particularly subtle "double," one that doubtless consisted of the "super-physical" Soul Body only.

G. DESCRIPTIONS BY AUSTRALIAN ABORIGINES OF THE "SILVER CORDS" OF THEIR "CLEVER MEN"

Dr. Donald Rose[179] learned from Australian aborigines of their initiation ceremonies. The account includes the following statements: "A man . . . lay on his back. . . . From his mouth the boys saw a thing come forth, a living thing that was not a snake or a cord—but *it looked like a cord and moved like a snake. Slowly it issued . . . the length of a man's finger but not so thick. It became almost as long as his arm. It left his mouth and crawled in the grass, then.*

"The remaining lad said the 'clever men' [= "physical" mediums] lay on their backs and that '*clever ropes extruded from their mouths and their navels.*'"

"Half the aborigines interviewed maintained that they had seen '*a magic cord*' under these circumstances. One described it as usually black [indicating low vitality], though sometimes sandy and never thicker than a horsehair. Another said that *the 'cords' looked 'like black cobwebs'* and crawled on the 'clever man's' face [a description which recalls the "cords" of Western "physical" mediums]."

Dr. Rose summarized the statements he had obtained from the aborigines as follows: *"Mostly, the 'cord' was inches rather than feet long, and two feet at most. The 'cord' is sandy to black, very thin rather than thick, and seemed to be alive."*

Statements similar to those made by Dr. Rose were attributed to the Professor of Anthropology at Sydney University, N.S.W., Australia—Professor A. P. Elkin. According to Colin Simpson,[180] Professor Elkin published a book entitled *Aboriginal Men of High Degree* (which we have not seen and of which Simpson gives neither the publisher nor the date). "In south-east Australia a spirit opens the postulate's side, inserts magical quartz crystals . . . and he then visits the sky and converses with ghosts and spirits; or a magical cord is inserted, as well as the quartz crystals, and *he is taken up to the sky on such a cord. . . . In the Kimberleys he also goes up to the sky on a cord or on the rainbow."* [*It is, of course, his own "silver cord"-extension which forms as the "double" separates from the body—and which is reabsorbed as the two reassociate.*] Professor Elkin was then quoted verbatim—and his pronouncement agrees with that of Professor M. Eliade: "Aboriginal medicine-men, so far from being rogues, charlatans and ignoramuses, are *men of high degree;* that is, men who have taken a degree in the secret life beyond that taken by most adult males . . . men of respected, and often outstanding, personality . . . of immense social significance, the psychological health of the group largely depending on faith in their powers. More and more anthropologists are coming to identical conclusions regarding the medicine-men of many widely separated countries. Psychologists and parapsychologists are also according them due respect. The drug houses send scouts to learn their medical secrets. . . ."

It will be evident that very similar "cords" were described in very different circumstances; namely (a) by people who had temporary out-of-the-body experiences and who saw and described their own "cords"; (b) by people who observed the "cords" of others, who were in course of leaving the body permanently; (c) by prehistoric people and illiterates who evidently had temporary out-of-the-body experiences; (d) by other illiterate primitives who observed the "cords" of people who were in course of transition; (e) by observers of the phenomena of materialization; and (f) by Australian aborigines who watched "physical phenomena" produced by their "clever men" (mediums).

These "silver cords" were not imagined: In the first place, some (namely, those of certain materializations) have been photographed; in the second place, some were seen collectively; in the third place, dozens of people in different circumstances do not imagine the same things—or their occurrence in the same series of events. These "cords" were objective phenomena, extensions between the vacated physical body and the released, objective "double." There is thus ample evidence of the possibility envisaged by Professor Ducasse that the "doubles" of astral projectors do, indeed, bear extensions which have so often been compared to cords, threads, ropes, tapes, ribbons, strings, and beams or shafts of light.

H. THE REABSORPTION OF THE "CORD" AS THE "DOUBLE" REENTERS THE BODY

As already said, Turvey observed that his "cord" formed as his "double" quitted his body, and that it was reabsorbed as it reentered the body. Those who left the body and reentered it (those who still "lived") describe an event, namely, the reabsorption of the "cord," which others who left the body *and failed to reenter it (those who died)* never describe. This matter is considered in detail in *The Techniques of Astral Projection,* 1964 (p. 26) and *More Astral Projections,* 1964 (p. 129).

On the other hand, the dead describe an event which no astral projector describes: namely, the snapping, breaking, or "loosing" of the "cord" (see Appendix III).

VIII. *The Level of Consciousness*

The nonmediums who comprise Group I A (and whose "doubles" are interpreted as consisting of the "superphysical Soul Body only) never describe their consciousness (a) as having been dual, or (b) as waxing and waning, or (c) as "sub-normal" (that is, dreamy, confused, and fearful). They describe it as "super-normal" (that is, intense, clear, expansive, and often including clairvoyant activities). On the other hand, the mediumistically constituted persons who form Group IV (and whose "doubles" are interpreted as consisting not only of the "super-physical" Soul Body but also part of the "semi-physical" vehicle of vitality) describe first a period in which consciousness was (a) dual, (b) waxing and waning in intensity, and (c) "sub-normal" in general, followed (after the second "death") by a "super-normal" level with clairvoyance. The two stages in the total bodily constitution of the "double" are correlated with the two periods, each of which has a distinctive level of consciousness.

As was pointed out in the Introduction, Professor H. H. Price suggested that cases of astral travel might be regarded as observations of, or operations with, a subtle ("astral," "etheric," "physical," or "Soul") Body. Our evidence shows that this suggestion is amply justified by the facts included in numerous independent testimonies. The only exceptions are the cases that comprise Group I B—Second Part (the "doubles" cited in Group I B are interpreted as consisting of nothing but part of the "semi-physical" vehicle of vitality—which is merely a "bridge" between the Soul Body and the physical body and not, like the Soul Body, a separate instrument of consciousness).

IX. *Repercussion as the "Doubles" Reentered the Body*

This provides another indication as to the difference between the "doubles" that consist of the Soul Body only and those that are composite. In the former, the rapid and sudden return of the "double" rarely resulted in shock and repercussion; and the sudden return was not due to physical causes, such as a loud noise, but to mental causes, chiefly fear. In the latter, shock and repercussion were common, very severe, and due not only to the emotions but also to physical causes, especially sudden loud noises. (The former "doubles" were interpreted as containing some of the "semi-physical" vehicle of vitality, the latter as containing a significant amount of it.)

Our study amply confirms the opinion published by Dr. Hereward Carrington in his Introduction to Muldoon's *The Projection of the Astral Body:* "Any impartial reader will agree, I think, with the conclusion that it would be impossible for Mr. Muldoon to have written as he has—to have acquired this knowledge—without in some sense *experiencing* what he claims to have experienced. . . . His knowledge has been gained at first-hand, and as a result of actual experiment; that is very evident." Mr. Muldoon deserves the gratitude of all who are interested in psychic matters, for what is popularly called astral projection is a key to numerous problems of the first importance. His work can scarcely be overpraised.

Carrington noted that a number of people drew distinctions between man's various nonphysical bodies. He considered, "For the present purpose we may ignore these distinctions and speak of the 'astral body.' " Unfortunately, this confused the issue. Because of a failure to distinguish between the "semi-physical" vehicle of vitality (we repeat—a "bridge" but not a separate instrument of consciousness) and the "super-physical" Soul Body (the primary vehicle of consciousness), many apparent discrepancies remained. Among these were questions as to why some "doubles" could, and others could not, move a physical object; why some could, and others could not, pass through walls; why some could go far away from the physical body and others could not; why some "silver cord"-extensions were attached to the solar plexus while others were attached to the head.

We congratulate Mr. Muldoon on his outstanding work. But we do not agree that indiscriminate attempts should be made to experience projection. As already said, they will come when one is "ready" without being forced in the slightest degree. Those who force them may bitterly regret it.

Yet one understands Mr. Muldoon's recommendation. Benjamin Whichcote, Provost of King's, said, "If you say you have a revelation, I must have a revelation too before I can believe you." The only alternative method is to study the facts of experience that are reported by Muldoon and all the others who claimed to have had out-of-the-body experiences, to subject them to different kinds of logical and psychological analysis, and to see which hypothesis best explains them. We believe the results to be unanswerable. When all the books of a firm add up correctly in all directions we rightly regard that firm as sound. When our conception of a fossilized stem is based on sections taken through it in three directions at right angles to each other, it must be the correct correlation: All the component tissues and their interrelationships are known. Our judgment of out-of-the-body experiences is based on analyses of hundreds of testimonies from quite different points of view—on different conditions under which "doubles" are released (natural or enforced), on different kinds of people (mediumistic and nonmediumistic) who released their "doubles," and on different num-

bers of stages in the release—also of the reentry of
"doubles." We venture to believe that the results are
acceptable. Any other explanation would violate the
principle of economy of hypotheses—it would demand
hundreds of hypotheses.

"Doubles" that are no more than mental images doubtless occur, and "doubles" that represent "archetypes"
possibly occur: It is impossible to "prove" a negative
proposition—but *all the evidence goes to show that many
"doubles," in particular those considered in these pages,
were objective; some were "super-physical" in nature,
others were "semi-physical," and still others were an
admixture of both natures.*

INTERMEDIATE
(*More or Less Indefinite*)
CASES

N.B. These cases are not essential to our argument: They are mentioned to complete the account. The differences between mediumistic and nonmediumistic persons, between healthy and more or less sick people, are neither sharp nor permanent. For example, nonmediums may be temporarily mediumistic when ill. It would be strange if the entire testimonies of out-of-the-body experiences could be sharply divided into two groups—those in which the "double" was released in one stage (and reentered in one stage) and those in which it was released in two stages (and reentered in two stages).

"DOUBLES" GENERALLY
RELEASED IN A SINGLE STAGE
(SOMETIMES WITH A HINT
OF SECOND-STAGE RETURN)

Facts:

1. In these cases (Nos. 1–19, 21, 22, 24, 26, 28–30, 32–39, 45, 120–53, 286–93, 384, 387, 393, 396, 397, 400, 402, 404, 406,

409, 413, 415, 418, 423, 427, 429, 434, 438, 446, 454, 456—
187 cases) the "doubles" were also formed in a single stage.
2. The "doubles" were usually seen by the persons concerned.
3. The persons concerned were *either* of the mediumistic *or* nonmediumistic bodily constitution.
4. They were suffering from the effects of great exhaustion, grave illnesses, severe shock, a fall, sedative drugs, partial suffocation (including drowning), anesthetics, etc.
5. The "doubles" were luminous, subtle, and tenuous (rather than apparently solid and dead).
6. They were used by their owners as instruments of consciousness.

Hypotheses:

In the circumstances indicated, it was not the "super-physical Soul Body alone that was projected or the "semi-physical" vehicle of vitality alone, but part of the latter as well as the former; these "doubles" were composite. Characteristically, they remained composite, with the vehicle of vitality—which is not in itself an instrument of consciousness—more or less enveiling or enshrouding the Soul Body, the primary instrument of consciousness.

GROUP IB OF "DOUBLES"
("*Semi-Physical*" *Vehicles of Vitality*)

(This type of projection was not exemplified in *The Study and Practice of Astral Projection*, 1961, or in *More Astral Projections*, 1964.)

Case No. 403—R. P. Roberts[181]

"When I was an apprentice in a drapery establishment, I used to go to dinner at 12 and return at 12:30. . . . One day I went home to dinner at the usual hour. When I had partly finished I looked at the clock. To my astonishment it appeared that the time by the clock was 12:30. . . . I had only half finished my dinner and it was time for me to be back at the shop. I felt dubious, so in a few seconds had another look, when to my agreeable surprise I found I had been mistaken —it was only just turned 12:15. . . .

"I finished my dinner and returned to business at 12:30. On entering the shop I was accosted by Mrs. Owen, my employer's wife. She asked me rather sternly where I had been since my [released "double's"] return from dinner. I replied that I had come straight from dinner. A long discussion followed which brought out the following facts.

"About a quarter of an hour previous to my actually entering the shop (i.e., at about 12:15), I ["double"] was seen by Mr. and Mrs. Owen and a well-known customer (a Mrs. Jones) to walk into the shop, go behind a counter and place my hat on a peg. As I was going behind the counter, Mrs. Owen remarked, with the intention that I should hear, 'that I had arrived when I was not wanted!' This remark was prompted by the fact that, a few minutes previous, a customer was in the shop in want of an article which belonged to the stock under my charge, and which could not be found in my absence.

"As soon as this customer left, I ["double"] was seen to enter the shop. It was observed by Mr. and Mrs. Owen and Mrs. Jones that I did not appear to notice the remark made. In fact, I looked absent-minded and vague. Immediately after putting my hat on the peg, I returned to the same spot, put my hat on again, and walked out of the shop, still looking in a very mysterious manner. This incensed Mrs. Owen to say 'that my behaviour was very odd, and she wondered where I was off to.'

"I, of course, contradicted these statements. . . . This, however, availed nothing, and during our discussion the above-mentioned Mrs. Jones came into the shop again and was appealed to at once by Mr. and Mrs. Owen. She corroborated every word of their account and added that she saw my 'double' coming down Rating Row within a few yards of the shop in time to hear Mrs. Owen's remark about my coming too late. These three persons gave their statement of the affair quite independently of each other. There was no other person near my age in the Owens' employment, and there could be no reasonable doubt that my form had been seen by Mrs. Jones.

"They would not believe my story until my aunt, who had dined with me, said positively that I did not leave the table before my time was up. You will, no doubt, notice the coincidence. *At the moment when I felt, with a startling sensation, that I ought to be at the shop, and when Mr. and Mrs. Owen were extremely anxious that I should be there, I appeared to them, looking as they said, 'as if in a dream or in a state of somnambulism.'* " We interpret this case (as those of Mlle. Sagée, etc., if authentic) as a "double" that consisted of the "semi-physical" vehicle of vitality only. Had it included the "super-physical" Soul Body it would have exhibited intelligence and could have been used by Mr. Roberts to make observations which he might, or might not, have remembered on reentering his physical body. This was a "ghost"—of a "living" man.

Case No. 405—F. C. Coblentz[182]

Coblentz, the son of Professor V. Coblentz, of the New York College of Pharmacy, said, "I shall describe the occurrence as it actually took place. The incident came to pass on a Christmas Eve. The scene of my meeting with the ghost lies not in the usual moonlit isolated road, or in the lonely graveyard, but somewhat unconventionally in my own home.

"Having completed the adornment of a Christmas tree, I stepped into the library. . . . The hall clock struck the hour of six. Shortly after, my mother came to me from her boudoir and requested me to go and bring her a glass of water. Complying, I went to the pantry, obtained the water, and returned up the rear stairs. Upon reaching the head where the first landing of the front stairway is located, I saw my mother descending by the front way. I saw her plainly, as this portion of the house is well lighted. She was but six steps below me at the time. Immediately my words were, 'Mother, here is your glass of water.' There was no reply, nor any visible sign that she had even heard me. With my glass of water in hand, I followed down the stairs. Apparently once more I did not make myself heard, but by this time we were near the foot of the stairs, so I contented myself with waiting until we should reach the lower hall. Rather slowly and gracefully, my mother moved on, and I trailed not far behind.

"Now we had reached the hall. Here I made my offer of the water for the third time, in the same words as before, but with this addition: 'Why on earth don't you take it—where are you going?' She turned to the right then and, sweeping through the doorway of the parlour, she entered that room. . . . She was attired completely in white. . . .

"For a moment I stood in the hall, and watched her as she directed her steps about the parlour. I was of the opinion that she was searching for a match to light the gas. I stepped into the room to await the accomplishment of her purpose, and then I would once more proffer the water to my unheeding mother. I walked to the corner of the mantel. . . . Next I observed her move towards me. I said something to her about finding the matches. Hardly had I spoken before the outlines of her form grew blurred. . . . A suspicion came over me that something was not entirely just as it should be. . . . The next instant, as I made a quick step towards the form, it grew rapidly fainter. . . . The glass of water slipped from my grasp and crashed to the floor. I stared in utter amazement as the moving living object which I had followed and talked to was now nothing but a small, white, irregular vanishing form in the air. . . . I found my mother where I had left her. A thorough search . . . failed to reveal traces of earthly prowlers. . . ."

Case No. 432—A. W. Osborn[183]

Osborn provided a case that is very like those of Roberts and Coblentz. He saw his released "double": It was "as clear and objective" as the stairs which he, and it, were climbing. On another occasion, when his wife saw his released "double," Osborn was ill. Osborn observed, "I was not self-conscious in the 'double.'" In other words, his vehicle of vitality (unlike the Soul Body) was not an instrument of consciousness.

Case No. 431—Dr. W. Wynn Westcott[184]

In citing this case, the editor drew attention to its similarity to that which was printed in Gurney's *Phantasms of the Living.*[184] Westcott arranged to meet Mr. A. B. and the Reverend T. W. Lemon at the British Museum Reading Room at 10:45 A.M. the next morning. However, he had a cold on Thursday and was confined to bed, "fretting at not being able to keep the appointment." Thus, his attention was directed to the Reading Room and his friends therein (although the physical body was incapacitated, his "double" was not). The account continues:

"I heard subsequently from Mr. A. B. personally that he and the Rev. T. W. Lemon had met at the Reading Room and had not been able to find me, but that he had asked some officials, notably one named Ryan, for me, and some habitués among the readers, notably a Miss O'Connell and a Mrs. Salmon. Mr. A. B. also said that Ryan and Mrs. Salmon had both told him that they had seen me in the Reading Room, walking around as if seeking someone, just before he enquired of them.

"A few days after that I went to the Reading Room and saw Miss O'Connell and Mrs. Salmon, when the latter, in a jocular way, said, 'Is it *really* you today, or not?' She was so much impressed by the peculiarity of my appearance on the 13th that for a long time she made the same jocular query when I met her. Miss O'Connell was told of the event at that time, and has repeatedly heard Mrs. Salmon and me refer to the incident." These statements were corroborated.

Case No. 432—J. F. C. Arthur Hamilton Boyd[185]

Boyd, of Edinburgh, sat in his club, slept and "dreamed" that he was running to his home, fearing he was late for dinner. The case is here abbreviated.

"I opened the door with my latch-key and hurried upstairs to dress; about half-way up I looked down and saw my father standing in the hall, looking up at me. At this point I awoke, and, finding that it was a few minutes past twelve P.M., I rose immediately from my chair and went home. On my arrival, I was astonished to find that the house was lighted up and my father and one of my brothers searching the rooms and calling for me.

"My father, on seeing me, expressed much surprise and asked whence I had come. I explained that I had only just returned from the Club. He then asked me if I had not come in about twelve o'clock, and, on my replying in the negative, told me the following facts.

"He had, as was his custom, been sitting in his smoking-room and, about twelve, rose from his chair intending to go to bed. On opening the door which led into the hall, he heard the front door shut, and distinctly saw me hurriedly cross the hall and run upstairs, and, looking up, saw me glance down at him and disappear. He went to his room and remarked to my mother that he had locked the front door as I had come in. My mother said she thought he must be mistaken, for, had I returned, I would not have passed her room without wishing her goodnight. My father confidently affirmed that he had seen me enter the house, but, as my mother was still unconvinced, he went to my room and, finding it unoccupied, he called my brother and began to search

for me. While they were thus engaged I actually returned.
. . . It was some time before I could convince him that I had
only just returned."

Case No. 433—J. P. Challacombe[186]

Challacombe, at school in Devon, had retired to bed about
9:30 or 10:00 P.M. but could not sleep, thinking especially of
his mother. The testimony continues: "My bed was so placed
that I could see the staircase, and after a bit, to my surprise,
I heard someone coming up the stairs. It flashed into my
mind that it was mother, and so it proved to be. She was
dressed in a black dress that I had never seen before, and had
on her pink shawl and gold chain, and as she came into the
room her shoes creaked; in fact they did so all the time. I did
not feel at all frightened, but tried to get out of bed to go to
her; but something held me back. She went to the bed before
mine, where my chum sleeps, and bent over and looked at
him. Then she came to me and kissed me: I tried to kiss her,
but could not. Then she disappeared and seemed to vanish
in a mist. . . . I am quite sure that I was awake, and saw every
object in the room when she was there."

This narrative was corroborated by Challacombe's mother,
who said, "The queer part is that, at the time, I was visiting a
cousin in Wales, and Jack knew nothing about it. The evening he speaks of, I had returned home and had removed all
my walking things, with the exception of my boots, dress and
watch-chain. My dress Jack had never seen, and I am not in
the habit of wearing my chain outside my dress. As for the
boots, they were a pair I had not worn for years because they
were in the habit of creaking.

"I went to the door to wait for my cousin, who was a long
time saying goodnight to a friend, and while I was there
I was thinking deeply of Jack as I had not received his morn-

ing letter. We made an agreement that when he went to boarding-school we would think of one another every night and also say 'goodnight.' "

Case No. 435—Miss M. E. "Stanley" and Mrs. "Stanley"

This case was published in the *Journal of the Society for Psychical Research*.[187] As with numerous others, the sight of the "double" of Miss "Stanley" by her mother was due to the direction of the former's attention to the latter. "My mother was ill and I was tending her in our little flat. . . . A friend asked me to go to a theatre with her. . . . Having settled mother for the night, I was ready to go, and my mother said, 'Now, Marjorie, do *not* come to me when you come home to-night unless I call you,' and I said I would not go in. At 11:30 P.M., my friend Miss M. said before we parted, 'Do come in to have some refreshment. . . .' I said, 'No, thank you, I think I must go straight home, as my mother might wake up and be anxious if she found I was not in.' But Miss M. persisted in asking me . . . and I ended in going . . . I stayed out about an hour and went quietly to bed on my return.

"Imagine my amazement when, the next morning, the first thing my mother asked me was, 'Marjorie, why did you come in to see me last night when I asked you not to?' Of course, I told her I had not thought of going to her, as that had been arranged. She said she saw me come in, bend over her, as I had often done—without speaking. . . . Then I went out. . . . "

Case No. 436—Miss M. E. "Stanley" and Miss "Florence"[187]

This case followed the last cited. Miss "Stanley" visited a house where several ladies were staying. She said, "One was a stranger to me but we spoke, and she, in a very jaunty way, told me how ill she was after many operations; aged 69, what could you expect, etc. . . . I was so amazed at such faith . . . that I exclaimed, 'I have never seen such marvellous faith!' and was about to leave the room when I turned to someone and said, 'You have not told me this lady's name.' I was told the name and I left the house. I must add here that I have great faith in healing through the power of the Spirit of God and that night, in my silence to God, I urgently pleaded for the healing of this woman, and she was very vividly in my mind, with all her sufferings, as I asked for her.

"Two days later I went again to the Convalescent Home and . . . went up and asked how she was. Her reply was, 'Did you pray for me the other night?' I said, 'Yes, I did.' She said, 'I thought you had, for you came into my room and you looked just as you do now. I felt vibrations coming from you and I felt better and happier—and you vanished.' "

These two testimonies were corroborated by Mrs. "Stanley" and Miss "Florence" respectively.

Case No. 440—E. Ernest Hunt[188]

This case concerned Hunt's brother and represented another instance of projection due to directed attention. "His wife was practically dying in a fever hospital. . . . Her husband, three miles away, was naturally worried. The night-nurse was frightened by 'someone' prowling around the building, and reported the matter. When the husband went to the hospital the next day, the night-nurse confronted him, 'You are the man!' Yet the husband had never been out of his house the night before."

Case No. 442—Mr. "Ed"[189]

Dr. E. Mueller[189] stated: "One of my acquaintances, walking in the street, felt somebody overtaking him from behind and, turning his head, saw his 'double' walking beside him . . . ; as he looked at it intently, it disappeared." This case reminds one of a certain English professor whose often-released "double" was several times seen by his students. He was thought to be "haunted" and, of course, quite unnecessarily avoided by some. It is also like the case of the lady journalist, cited above.

Case No. 459—Edith M. Wood[190]

Mrs. Wood said, "One day I was coming downstairs. I saw my own spirit-form coming down with me, by my side. I did not understand it at the time, nor now—I only know that I walked downstairs with myself!" (The lady was able to produce "raps" and other "physical" phenomena—i.e., her "double" was loose and projectable: It remained near the body and made movements that were identical with those of the body. There was no consciousness via this "double." Her physical movements probably released it.)

Later,[191] Mrs. Wood described a similar experience: "I had been frying some bacon [? the fumes caused the release of the loose "double"]. I called to my daughter, 'Go for the doctor —I am dying!' Then I called to God, 'Not yet! Not yet! My child!' After I had uttered my prayer I saw that, *about three feet* away from me, stood my spirit-form. As I prayed it moved towards my side and entered my body again. Then I gradually began to see light, and I knew I had been very near 'passing away.' It was all wonderful. I could not explain the experience."

The person who released this type of "double" was invariably quite unaware of doing so, and he made no observations as to any phenomena (such as the presence or absence of "mist," a review of his past life, or a "blackout," which occur in all the other types of account). Most significantly, he did not use his released "double" as an instrument of consciousness (which occurs to a variable extent in all our other groups). He did not see his own "silver cord"-extension, his own vacated physical body, or the environment corresponding to his "double." There was no consciousness at all, either of, or through, this released "double." The facts agree with the statements of clairvoyants (for example, C. W. Leadbeater) to the effect that the vehicle of vitality—unlike the Soul Body—is not a separate instrument of consciousness. This statement is supported by numerous observations that, where part of the vehicle of vitality accompanies the released Soul Body, it causes some enshroudment of consciousness and some dimming of the environment.

A number of these "doubles" were seen collectively, and these cannot be explained as telepathic mental images (or "archetypes") unless further additional hypotheses are advanced. Moreover, the person concerned was not thinking of (visualizing) himself; on the contrary, he was concerned with a distant person or place. In the latter circumstances his more or less "loose" "double" followed the direction of his attention (as occurs with the "doubles" in our other groups, concerning which there are other reasons for concluding they are not mere mental images or "archetypes").

While not doubting that telepathed mental images do occur, we maintain that the mental image hypothesis (and the "archetype" hypothesis) does not apply to these cases: These "doubles" were objective, "semi-physical" in nature.

COMPARABLE "COMMUNICATIONS"

(Comparisons of the first-hand testimonies cited above—concerning temporary releases from the body—with "communications" concerning permanent releases)

It will be evident that if (a) the first-hand testimonies of the many astral projectors concerning their temporary release from the body, summarized on pp. 100–2 correspond to fact and if (b) these "doubles" are objective and if (c) the "communications" of the hundreds of the supposed dead who (necessarily via mediums) described their permanent release from the body are reliable, there should be a general resemblance between the two quite distinct sets of accounts—*and a particularly close resemblance would be expected between the mediumistic projectors (whose "doubles" were definitely composite, with a significant portion of the vehicle of vitality), and "communications" concerning the process of permanent discarnation. "Communicators" are unanimous in stating that the death of the physical body involves the release of the whole of the vehicle of vitality. In other*

*words, the immediate after-death "double" was always com-
posite. Clairvoyants observe that, whereas living bodies have
an aura, (d) corpses have none.*

1. *Many people who were temporarily discarnate observed
that their Soul Bodies left via the head.* In *The Supreme Adventure*[192] we cited the "communicator" Heslop as stating
that in permanent discarnation "the process begins at the
feet . . . and emerges from the head."

2. *Mediumistically constituted people released a "double"
that was interpreted as including part of the vehicle of vitality; they saw "mist," etc., leave their bodies.* It formed part
of the "double," enshrouding the Soul Body, and therefore
affected their contact with the environment. Similarly, a
"communicator," "H. J. L.," told J. S. M. Ward[193] that the
landscape seemed "shrouded in mist," and Dr. F. H. Wood[194]
described "a grey mist-land or state." The "communicator" of
A. L. E. H.[195] spoke of "a veil." The four "communicators"
of Geraldine Cummins,[196] that of the anonymous Letters
from Hell.[197] F. W. Fitzsimons[198] and "Marmaduke"[199] described "mist." Lord Dowding's "communicator" spoke of
"fog," and W. T. Stead's[200] of "thick clouds."

3. *Many who temporarily left the body described having
experienced, at quite an early stage in the process, a nonemotional review of their past lives.* The same statement was
commonly made by "communicators" in describing what had
happened when they died. In *The Supreme Adventure*[201]
we cited the following "communications": "My entire life
un-reeled itself." "Everything we have done comes before us
as a present memory." "I saw my life unfold before me in a
procession of images." "I seemed to be seeing pictures of my
life." "I reviewed my life as though I had no responsibility
for it." Dr. Karl A. Wickland[202] received the following "communication": "Every act of my past stands before me." Swami

Omananda Puri[203] said, "At death man sees his life and re-lives it as a whole." In Norway, the "communicator" of Judge Dahl[204] spoke of a "kaleidoscope"—the "new arrival" saw "rolled-up pictures" of the past earth-life. The "communica-tor" of Charlotte G. Herbine[205] said, "The whole of my life passed before me like a panorama."

4. *Many who left the body temporarily observed that, as the "double" separated from the body, there was a "blackout" (or "tunnel"-effect) in consciousness:* If the process of separa-tion was relatively slow, then they seemed to go through a dark "tunnel," "passage," "corridor," or "cave." Exactly the same was said by "communicators" in describing their deaths: In *The Supreme Adventure*[206] we cited "a cave," "a tunnel," and "a dark tunnel."

5. *As already said, those projectors whose "doubles" we interpreted as consisting of the "super-physical" Soul Body (our Group I A) did not report seeing "mist," or having sub-normal consciousness, or meeting "hinderers," etc. (i.e., they did not report signs of the "Hades" environment): On the other hand, mediumistic people, whose "doubles" gave evi-dence of containing a significant portion of the "semi-physical" vehicle of vitality, characteristically reported these things.* Moreover, the latter represent those mortals whose re-leased "doubles" would presumably most nearly correspond to those of the newly dead: These, it is said, tend to sleep and dream (on account of the enshroudment of the Soul Body by the vehicle of vitality—an enshroudment that is here necessarily greater than with mediumistic mortals, since death involves the release of *the whole* of the vehicle of vitality, bringing a maximum degree of enshroudment).

A "communicator" of Charlotte G. Herbine[207] described his own "passing" as follows: "All became black ["blackout"]. A curious feeling of *rushing waters* [= the loosening of the vehicle of vitality]; then the scene changed. . . . I had two bodies, one on the ground and the other standing. I said, 'Well, that's me physical dead—and that's me "double" here!' "

A "communicator" who confessed that he had lived "without faith, following no aim, living but to enjoy the moment," had, on dying, found himself "earthbound." The descriptions he gave correspond to those of the astral projectors who contacted "Hades" conditions. The account is in *Letters from Hell*.[208] Immediately after death he found himself in "mist." After a time, through the mist, he saw "human phantoms flitting along." These were obviously not helpers, and he "viewed them with horror." They surrounded him and tried to detain him; thus they were "hinderers." The already dim light became dimmer until "it was a mere ghost of a radiance." He thought, "This, then, is what I have come to—I had died and found myself in 'Hades'. . . . How shall I describe the darkness? It oppresses as with the weight of centuries: it is as though one were wedged in between mountains."

He then experienced the first review of his past life. He said, "My sins! What boots it now to remember them, but I must, I must. The life of sin is behind me, finished and closed. But with fearful distinctness it lies open to my vision, as a page to be read . . . in all its minutest parts. . . . A thousand trivial things—not trifles here, though I once believed them such—raise their front in bitter accusation. Life lies before me as an open book, a record of minutest detail. . . . I live over again the whole of my earthly life. . . . Hades has *a river,* the waters of which are heavy, dark and muddy . . . it is fed by the falsehood and injustice of the world: every lie, every wrong, helps to swell it. That is why its waters are so turbid, so fearfully foul. . . . There are men who rush through life in a whirl of amusement; others sleep through it, others again wear themselves out for its paltry amenities, calling that 'to live,' forsooth! Oh, could I live over again but a single year of my earthly span!"

This idea—that the "Hades" belt of the earth, the "misty," "foggy," or "watery" region, is rendered impure by the base thoughts and emotions that are given out by mortals—is often communicated. The "communicator" of Mary Bruce Wallace[209] called it "a curtain of darkness" which enfolds the earth, and said that mortals may cooperate with helpful spirits in cleansing it.

Many "communicators" say that the sometimes unpleasant "Hades" environment, with its possible "hinderers," must be "crossed" by certain astral projectors (those with the mediumistic bodily constitution) and by all who die. The matter of "hinderers" was mentioned by the "communicators" of the American, Mrs. Keeler (see *The Techniques of Astral Projection,* pp. 18–22). They may use the method described by the Danish "communicator" cited above—they may "surround" one and so bar one's way. In France, "Reine" (Cornillier)[210] said that they "surrounded" her newly released "double" and "formed a barrier"—and they "mocked" her.

"Hades" conditions (through which the average person who dies in old age sleeps) may be unpleasant, even dangerous, for those who are awake in it—especially if they harbor evil thoughts and emotions. This is one of the reasons that all and sundry should *not* attempt promiscuous projections (or undertake the development of "possession" mediumship).

"Paradise" conditions, on the other hand (entered after the second "death"), abound in willing and powerful helpers (see *The Techniques of Astral Projection*).

A "communicator" of J. S. M. Ward's[211] described his second "death" as follows: "A great weight seemed to crush me. My surroundings began to blur. I shrieked to my guide,

'Help me to get clear of this weight!' He held out his hand and I found myself free [from the hitherto enshrouding vehicle of vitality]. Then my astral shell [shed at the second "death"] whirled out of sight . . . and I saw a beautiful landscape. I had reached the plane of the spiritual [Soul] Body."

"Claude," communicating (Mrs. Kelway Bamber)[212] gave a typical description of the reverse of the second "death" when he returned from "Paradise" to speak to his mother. He said, "I passed with two friends through the Astral Plane [= "Hades"] to the earth. As we came nearer, *the atmosphere became thicker and misty* and the houses, etc., seemed indistinct. The view disappeared and I found myself in your room." "Claude" also mentioned the unpleasant condition of the "Hades" atmosphere, due to the evil thoughts and emotions of men. He described "what looks like a thick grey mist, caused by the thoughts of cruelty, rage, grief and pain that are continuously outpouring."

"Marmaduke"[213] described "Hades" conditions as "the grey mists of the lower world" and said they were inhabited by "those who are still sunk in their old earth sins—the earthbound spirits."

6. Many projectors stated that they saw (a) their own bodies and (b) dead friends. The supposed dead, communicating, make these statements. Moreover, many projectors said that they did not, at first, realize that they were out of their bodies (in the "double"), and the "dead" say the same: There is a duplicate *world,* as well as a duplicate *body,* and the similarities may at first obscure the differences that obtain.

7. *Certain projectors observed that their newly released "doubles" were in a horizontal position not far above the body. The same is said by certain "communicators."* For example, in *The Supreme Adventure*[214] we cited "Heslop" as communicating the statement that "generally" the "double"

"floats horizontally above the dying form." A "communicator" told F. W. Fitzsimons[215] that he "floated horizontally" above his body. Another told F. T. Robertson[216] that his newly released "double" was "parallel" over his corpse. Such an initial position would hardly be expected.

8. *Many who claimed to have left their bodies temporarily also claimed to see their own "silver cord"-extensions.* Their testimonies are supported by a number of people who, observing the process of quitting the body permanently, claimed to see the "silver cord"-extensions of others. For example, Dr. Hout reported seeing "a silver-like substance or cord" (which "snapped"); Oaten, "a psychic umbilical cord" (which "snapped"); Florence Marryat, "cords of light, like electricity" (which "ruptured"); and Mr. "G" "a cord" (which became "severed").

"Communicators" who purport to describe the process by which they themselves quitted the body permanently give identical accounts.

In Great Britain, F. T. Robertson,[216] cited a relative who said, "A cord from the solar plexus was the link which held me to my old body. . . . Then I saw that the cord had snapped. I was free—a new man, a new body, born again!" "H. J. L." told J. S. M. Ward:[217] "From my mouth came, as it were, a cord of light. It snapped." "Edgar," communicating to the Reverend C. Drayton Thomas,[218] told him that, immediately after he died, he would "rest awhile until the etheric cord is broken—a process that may take a day or two." "Myers," communicating to Geraldine Cummins,[219] mentioned two "silver cords"—one (evidently that which was an extension of the vehicle of vitality) was attached to the solar plexus, while the other (evidently that which was an extension of the Soul Body) was attached to the head. An earlier "communicator" of Miss Cummins's,[220] like the clairvoyant Oaten, called it "an umbilical cord."

In America, Mrs. A. L. Fernie's[221] "communicator" sp
of a "cord" which became severed—the last act in the p
ess of dying. Mrs. M. E. Longley, in describing the sa
process, said, "Now there is only a slight attachment by
'silver cord' which has become very thread-like and att
uated . . . until the 'cord' is entirely 'loosed.' "

In South Africa, F. W. Fitzsimons[222] described "a magn
cord" which became "severed" and so "freed the spirit c
pletely."

In Italy, A. Farnese[223] received a description purporting
come from a man who had been a sensualist. Released fr
his body, he saw a lady whom he knew (and toward wh
he had directed his attention). He tried to follow her. "B
he stated, "I could not. It was as if a great chain [the "si
cord"] held me fast. I could not go more than a few ya
from my body [because the released "double" included
vehicle of vitality]. And then I saw why. A 'chain' of d
silk—it seemed no thicker than a spider's web—held me
my body." Later, he saw this "thread" was "loosed." (Eccl
astes [xii, 6] said, "Or ever the silver cord be loosed. .
Then shall the dust return to the earth as it was, and
spirit shall return to God Who gave it.")

We have noted that Mrs. Cripps and Mrs. Porter in Brita
S. J. Muldoon in America, Badenhorst in South Africa, a
others, all observed that so long as their "doubles" were n
their bodies, and therefore included a significant portion
the vehicle of vitality, vital forces could be seen pulsating
that feature: It was the equivalent of the umbilical cord
childbirth. "Vettellini," communicating to P. E. Cornil
(p. 387) stated that the amount of energy that we obtain fr
food is insufficient for our needs—that there is also "
breath of the vital, cosmic force" and he added, "This i
universal law, governing all living creatures." He sta
"This sortie of the astral body [vehicle of vitality] for

purpose of gathering nourishment [cosmic vitality] necessary to organic life is not to be confounded with the disengagement [of the Soul Body] of highly evolved human beings in quest of information or influences [i.e., in quest of helpers from "Paradise" conditions] that may develop their consciousness. *The first [the absorption of cosmic vitality] is common to everything that lives [= plants, animals, and men]; the second [the projection of the Soul Body] is the privilege of a human Spirit who has already attained a high degree of spiritual development."*

As already said, the descriptions provided by clairvoyants are in absolute accord with "communications" such as are exemplified above. The descriptions of astral projectors are also concordant. Mrs. Annie Brittain,[224] while out of her body, visited a woman who was dying. She saw "a deep-violet aura or mist" around the dying body. Her discarnate helper told her that such a "mist" (= the released vehicle of vitality) is observed (by discarnates and—as we have shown—by certain incarnates) "whenever a spirit is leaving the body." He added, "There is always intense activity of the *vital electricity* [*in the vehicle of vitality*] . . . and it is this intensity of vibration which produces the violet tone." Then Mrs. Brittain "saw the violet deepening round *the head*" and "the discharge of sparks grew more rapid, till," she said, "gradually above the body I saw an exact replica of the old body, clothed in light. This counterpart rose until it was about *eight to nine inches* clear of the old body. . . . Her [discarnate] mother drew near and touched the ethereal form above the bed. Then a most glorious awakening came—*a flash of light passed between the two bodies.* The mortal body collapsed, a lifeless corpse. The vital aura had gone and a dense grey mist enveloped the dead body."

9. *Many projectors discovered that when they directed their attention to a distant person or place it immediately*

went there. The same is said by many "communicators": They had left their bodies permanently, then thought of distant parents or friends and at once found themselves with them, observing, in some cases, their anxiety or grief but seldom being able to make themselves seen or heard.

The "communicator" of Duffey's *Heaven Revised* described how he died and found himself in an earthly valley, "glorified and spiritualised" (in "Paradise" conditions), and wondered where his spirit friends were. He said, "I was not conscious of having uttered a thought aloud, but as if in response to it, I found myself in the presence of two youths. . . ."

G. G. Andre[225] was urged by his "communicator" to "send out a ray of love" toward him: This, he said, would serve as a channel of communication through which the beneficent forces from the spirit world may reach him." Similarly, the "communicator" of W. S. Montgomery Smith[226] stated, "Love is the strongest link" between mortals and discarnate souls. He insisted: "It is the only way we can work for the benefit of mortals." The "communicator" of G. Trevor[227] told Trevor that he helped his two mortal brothers by his thoughts and prayers. "Wilberforce"[228] stated that while he was "united with the physical forces" (= vehicle of vitality, i.e., during the "Hades" period) he could easily help mortal friends, but later (after the second "death") he could not contact them unless and until, by their loving thoughts, they provided a "ladder."

"Stead"[229] communicated while still in "Hades." He said, "In this land we are much more sensitive than whilst on earth, and when thoughts are directed to us by mortals we have a direct call from those currents of thought thus generated. We are practically always able to come in close contact with the person who is thinking of us."

The "communicator" of Wilfred Brandon[230] said to all

who have some psychic ability: "Call upon us with your thoughts—prepare to do your part in co-operation." Speaking of men killed in battle,[231] he said, "Individual thoughts and prayers strongly projected, with concentration and the name of the beloved dead spoken, often reach their object. . . ."

Leon Denis[232] was told: "Our calls attract the attention of the deceased and facilitate their corporeal liberation [i.e., help them to pass through the second "death"]. Our ardent prayers . . . enlighten them."

In *The Supreme Adventure*[233] we cited "communications" concerning the direction of the attention by the dying (constituting a "call" to friends who had predeceased them).

10. *The level of consciousness permitted by the "doubles" of the living (given in our testimonies) corresponds to those of the "doubles" of the dead (given in "communications").* With mediumistic people (and with the newly dead) it was at first "subnormal" and restricted; later (after the vehicle of vitality had been shed) it became "supernormal," with telepathy, clairvoyance, etc.

11. *The phrase "the second 'death'" comes from "communicators," not from projectors; yet projectors clearly described the equivalent of the second "death."* This significant fact has hitherto been entirely overlooked. The fact is that, just as certain astral projectors—independently of mediumship—describe *a two-stage release of the "double,"* so the supposed dead, necessarily via mediums, describe the same process. What is more, the presumed condition is almost identical in the two cases, the one given in human testimonies and the other in "communications": The "doubles" of the living that have a two-stage release are interpreted as composite, as consisting of the Soul Body plus a significant portion of the vehicle of vitality; those of the dead are said to consist of the Soul Body plus the whole of the vehicle of

vitality. How, we ask, can this correspondence be explained on the hypothesis that these "doubles" were subjective (either mental images or "archetypes") in the minds of mortals?

In each case (the living and the dead) the facts are adequately explained on the hypotheses advanced: The vehicle of vitality at first more or less enshrouds the Soul Body, so that consciousness is more or less subnormal and restricted while "Hades" conditions are contacted. In such cases there is a second stage (the second "death") in which the Soul Body is freed from enshroudment so that consciousness becomes supernormal and "Paradise" conditions are glimpsed, if not fully entered.

The second "death" of "communicators" was considered in detail in *The Supreme Adventure*,[234] while the equivalent process, as described by people who had out-of-the-body experiences, was considered in detail in *The Next World—and the Next*.[235]

This is not all. The dead do not return and reinhabit a physical body. Astral projectors, on the other hand, do reinhabit their physical bodies, and it is surely significant that these people (quite unaware, of course, that they were providing highly evidential material) describe *the second "death" in reverse* (see *The Next World—and the Next*).[236]

The effects of the second "death" in reverse (though not, of course, the actual process) are described in significant terms by "communicators." Tim, a "communicator" who spoke through Mrs. Piper, stated, "I am talking, as it were, through a thick fog—and it often suffocates me. I can't get the right word—my mind is confused!" He had left "Paradise" and reentered "Hades" conditions in order to communicate. To do so, he had borrowed ectoplasm from the vehicle of vitality of the medium, i.e., he had reversed the second "death"—see *The Supreme Adventure*.[237] A child-communicator similarly said that, when he came "close to earth" it was "like fog." Later he spoke of "a hueless grey world." "Myers"[238] described it as "like diving into a black fog." "Muriel" communicating,[239] asked why, on one occasion, she encountered "a 'London' fog." "Muriel" also used the word "clouds" to describe the conditions. The "communicator" of A. L. E. H.[240] described "mist," and the "communicator" of Florence Dismore[241] alluded to "grey mists." Dr. Margaret Vivian's "communicator"[242] spoke of "a thick mist."

Identical descriptions are given by "communicators" who claimed not to make the full return journey from "Paradise" to earth (in order to communicate with mortals) but who said that they returned to the "Hades" region to help the "earthbound." Thus, "H. J. L.," communicating to J. S. M. Ward[243] in such circumstances described the landscape as "grey and shrouded in mist."

Not only so, but identical descriptions are given by people who were having an out-of-the-body experience, and who also claimed not to make the full return journey from "Paradise" to earth, but who said that they returned to the "Hades" region to help the "earthbound." Such a one was Mme. d'Espérance: She spoke of entering "a misty, cloudlike region" where she felt "stifled and cramped." Moreover, she was fully aware of the mechanism involved. She said I [in the Soul Body] must clothe myself with mist [from her own vehicle of vitality, rendering her "double" similar in composition to the "doubles" of the "earthbound"]. She said that she left "a world of radiant light" ("Paradise") and entered "a dim, shadowy world" ("Hades").

As we pointed out in *The Supreme Adventure*,[244] a number of eminent psychical researchers, including Dr. Richard Hodgson, Professor James Hyslop, Dr. Hereward Carrington, G. N. M. Tyrrell, and Dr. Raynor C. Johnson envisaged, as a working hypothesis in order to explain certain of the difficulties of communicating, the process which so many "com-

municators" describe and which we have shown to be ess
tially *the reverse of the second "death." They did not,*
course, mention this correspondence.

   It is surely significant that, just as certain *incarnate* So
namely, those who are mediumistic, claimed to pass throu
what is clearly *the equivalent of the second "death"* (
shedding of the vehicle of vitality—an experience that
commonly described by *discarnates*), so certain *discarna*
namely, those who return from "Paradise" conditions (
sorbing ectoplasm from the vehicle of vitality of an incarn
Soul) to communicate, describe passing through what
clearly *the reverse of the equivalent of the second "death."*
each case the fact that the "double" includes the substa
of the vehicle of vitality, obliges the person concerned
contact "Hades" conditions, described as "dim," "fogg
even "watery," and with more or less restricted conscic
ness.

   In any case, it will be evident that the first-hand *testimon*
concerning *temporary* releases of the "double" from the b
correspond in a remarkable fashion with *"communicatio*
concerning the *permanent* releases which we call death. 7
inference is obvious.

   12. *The movements of composite "doubles."* Apart fr
the concordance between the statements of those surviv
souls who manage verbally to *communicate* with suita
mortals and the observations made by astral projectors, th
are significant concordances between the behavior of cert
"ghosts" (*discarnates*)—those which we interpret as eit
consisting of, or including the vehicle of vitality—and th
incarnates with "doubles" of a similar constitution,
those that were composite. In both cases (as long as
"double" is composite) there is a tendency to the mechan
repetition of movements, to producing supernormal nois
a "ghost" will, for instance, repeatedly search for letters wh

he hid during life. Telekinetic effects and dual consciousness (i.e., some awareness of the physical body, and therefore the physical world, as well as the "double" and therefore the "Hades" environment) also occur in both conditions. Dual consciousness has, of course, some bearing on the question of cremation (see *The Supreme Adventure*[245] and *The Next World—and the Next*).[246] Again, just as mortals with composite "doubles" found that they could not move far away from their bodies—we cite "one," "two," "two or three," "three," and "six" feet in *More Astral Projections*—so the newly dead with composite "doubles" (for example, Franchezzo, cited above) make that statement. Complete release from the body comes only after the second "death."

To sum up this particular matter, whatever evidence exists for "ghosts" in the traditional sense is supported by the quite independent evidence for the existence of "ghosts" of living persons. The two lines of evidence provide mutual support.

THE STATUS OF THESE "COMMUNICATORS"

We have pointed out that the observations made by certain particularly able and reliable clairvoyants concerning the "semi-physical" vehicle of vitality, its nature and functions (for example, Phoebe Payne in 1938 and Mrs. Garrett in 1939) and the concordant observations and deductions of certain psychical researchers (for example, Herbert Bland, Dr. Raynor C. Johnson in 1955, and T. C. Lethbridge in 1961) had been forestalled by "communicators" decades before (for example, by those of Cora L. V. Tappan, 1875; Hoey, 1907; Morse, 1925; and Wingfield, 1925). In Germany, the "communicator" of Fr. J. Greber, a Roman Catholic priest who was quite unacquainted with psychic matters, made obviously significant statements. It is often difficult, for want of relevant data, to determine the nature of "communicators," but *these* cannot have been subconscious fragments of the total minds of the mediums concerned.

Numerous psychologists, psychical researchers, etc., have spent many years in carefully investigating the question posed centuries ago by Job (xiv, 14): "If a man die, shall he live again?" or does the Soul survive the death of the body? In a book entitled *Intimations of Immortality* we show that 81 percent became absolutely sure, 14 percent more or less sure, and only 4 percent remained doubtful. But there is a prior question, one which, if well-founded, renders Job's inquiry unnecessary. It is: "How does the Soul (with faculties that transcend time and space, such as telepathy, clairvoyance, and foreknowledge) manage to interact with the physical body (which exists in time and space)?

The answer is, we maintain, that interaction occurs between *the "super-physical" Soul Body* and *the physical body* because of the intermediate, interpenetrating *"semi-physical" vehicle of vitality:* This insures continuity between the Soul Body and the physical body so long as the latter lives.

Since the "communicators" cited above predated not only particularly reliable clairvoyants, but also particularly eminent psychical researchers in stating this extremely important matter, it is illogical to interpret them as mere fragments of the minds of (the quite unlettered) mediums concerned: Surely they represent Souls who have survived bodily death and managed to "get through" to humanity?

This conclusion is supported by the fact that other statements of these "communicators"—those concerning the nature of man and his relationship to God—are in absolute agreement with the statements of all the great British, German, French, Hindu, and other mystics (most, if not all, of whom were averse to the exercise of mediumship!).

Some Scriptural texts receive illumination from these studies: Jesus[247] said, "Whosoever drinks of the 'water' that I shall give him . . . will be *an inner spring welling-up for Eternal Life,*" and[248] "Whosoever believes in Me, as the Scripture says, '*streams*' of living '*waters*' shall flow out from *within him.*" Hence, He urged His followers, "*Dwell in Me, as I in you* [= *be consciously at-one with Me Who am the Life of your life, at the 'centre' of your innermost Self*]. No branch can bear fruit by itself, but only if it remains united with the vine: no more can you bear fruit unless you remain united with Me. I am the Vine and you are the branches. He who dwells in Me, as I in him, bears much fruit: for apart from Me you can do nothing. . . . *If you dwell in Me and My words in you, ask what you will and you shall have it.*" Apparent miracles of healing, etc.— primarily, of course, spiritual healing, the healing of the Soul—will be possible, since he who is at-one with Christ is a channel through which spiritual "waters" flow for the benefit of those who need them.

Many psychic experiences and phenomena lend support, at the evidential level, to these all-important spiritual activities. (a) Prescott Hall, a skeptic concerning all psychical matters, made a number of investigations. Among these was an attempt to check up on supposed out-of-the-body experiences: He obtained details of certain techniques that are said to facilitate *out-of-the-body experiences* and probably succeeded, at least in part; for he reported[249] that he observed his body to be "*blazing with streamers pouring in and out from the solar plexus.*" (b) Anna Maria Roos[250] described a similar phenomenon in connection with *mesmeric trance* (which represents an assisted, if not an enforced, out-of-the-body condition). She said, "Somnambulists (in mesmeric trance) generally notice a *radiation of 'light' from the hypnotiser* . . . encircling the hypnotiser's head like a halo; they see cones of rays emanating from his hands, also from his *solar plexus.* (c) Sylvan J. Muldoon[251] observed, "*When projected* (= *out of the body*) *in the Astral* (= *Soul*) *Body, one can observe this neuric and cosmic energy; that is, he can see its colour and condensation in the bodies of others. It is luminous, like white light. It is this energy which gives the Astral* [*Soul*] *Body its phosphorescent appearance.* . . . Although

the glow of the neuric energy can be seen throughout
entire body, *it is condensed mostly in the centre of the bo*
It is very luminous at the centre of the body—at the so
plexus region." (d) Miss Jeane Bradford, of Los Angeles, w
had an out-of-the-body experience, told me:[252] "I was lit
like a Christmas tree. I looked down at my arm and found
full of *streams of bright, neon-like light*." She later found t
E. S. Drower (*The Secret Adam*) mentioned the Manda
Nacoreans, "who hold a ceremony to create the Resurr
tion [= release the Soul] Body" and who chant, "*Oh,*
lovely radiance of the liver! Ah, the beautiful radiance
the heart! . . . or words to that effect." Mrs. Bradford co
mented, "I know just what they mean." (e) A writer in
London Forum[253] described out-of-the-body experiences t
he had had. He observed, "Breathing begins from the d
phragm . . . then ecstasy increases [= the Soul Body is
erated from the physical body] and *a sense of power po*
into the solar plexus." (f) Dr. Paul Gibier[254] told of an
graver whose Soul Body was forced out of his physical be
because of *suffocation from the fumes of an imperfectly bu*
ing oil-lamp. Although it was dark, he could see everyth
quite clearly: This, he said, was because of "*a ray of ligh*
that was emitted by his "epigastrium" (= *solar plex*
(g) The Reverend William Stainton Moses underwent *me*
umistic trance, another form of out-of-the-body state. He
several times observed that his hands were covered with
flame" and on one occasion *he "seemed to be on fire*." I
Guide ("Imperator") told him that the substance wh
caused the "flame" or "fire" was "*the vital principle*" and w
drawn from the spine and nerve centers principally (of
medium himself) and from all the sitters. Later, Stain
Moses was told that *his "light" was "fed from his bod*
Next morning he had pain over *the solar plexus*. (h) In o
of the most remarkable books ever written—*Swan on a Bl*

Sea, by Geraldine Cummins[256]—we find two references to this highly significant type of phenomenon. The "communicator," Mrs. Coombe Tennant, told how, when in the physical body, she had been present in a room, one of a trio who were listening to great music; the room was "peopled with the invisible dead." At first she felt, rather than saw, them, but one of the trio (A. J. Balfour) somehow provided "power" by means of which she saw a young woman (who had been Balfour's sweetheart) standing beside him. He was eighty years old and half-asleep (thus his "double" was partly released from his physical body and hence available to reinforce the psychic power of Mrs. Coombe Tennant and so to bridge the two worlds). *The young woman, Mary Catherine Lyttleton, who had died on Palm Sunday, 21st March, 1875, "literally shone down upon him as she stood beside him—rays of a hidden sun, as it were, emanating from her (Soul) Body. . . ."* The editor of Miss Cummins's book, Signe Toksvig, pointed out that on p. 85 of the Gerald Balfour study of Mrs. "Willett's" (= Mrs. Coombe Tennant's) mediumship,[257] the psychic was described as having seen a phantasm, "a lady in an old-fashioned dress, young and with thick, beautiful hair. She was standing beside the couch, *a brilliant 'light'* streaming round and from her whole figure. . . ." A third person was present, lying on a couch (evidently A. J. Balfour). (It may be added that Miss Cummins obtained the above-mentioned script on February 14, 1958, while the "Palm Sunday Case," containing the latter description, was not published until February, 1960, so that Miss Cummins was quite unaware that she was providing a remarkable corroboration of details that had been given in the also remarkable "Palm Sunday Case.")

REFERENCES

1. II Cor. xii, 2.
2. I Cor. xv, 35, 44.
3. Crookall, R., *More Astral Projections*, Aquarian Press, 1964, Case Nos. 44, 161–69, 224, 226, 238, 244, 247, 254, 259, 260, 268, 321, 370, 390.
4. Laubscher, Dr. B. J. F., *Where Mystery Dwells*, Bailey & Swinfen, 1963.
5. Eliade, Prof. M., *Shamanism*, Routledge, 1961.
6. Ref. No. 3, p. 146.
7. Muldoon, S. J. (and Hereward Carrington), *The Projection of the Astral Body*, Rider, 1929.
8. ———, *The Case for Astral Projection*, Aries Press, Chicago, 1936.
9. ——— (and Hereward Carrington), *The Phenomena of Astral Projection*, Rider, 1951.
10. Crowe, Catherine, *The Night Side of Nature* (1st ed., 1848), Routledge, 1904.
11. *Proc. S. P. R.*, 50, p. 169.
12. Crookall, R., *The Mechanisms of Astral Projection*, Darshana International, Moradabad, India, 1967.
13. ———, *The Supreme Adventure*, James Clarke, 1961.
14. ———, *The Study and Practice of Astral Projection*, Aquarian Press, 1961.
15. Hart, Prof. H., Parapsychology Monographs, No. 6, 1965; Parapsychology Foundation, Inc.
16. ———, *J. A. S. P. R.*, 1967, p. 75.
17. Jaffe, Dr. A., *Precognition and Apparitions*, University Books Inc., N.Y., 1965.
18. Ducasse, C. J., *A Critical Examination of the Belief in a Life After Death*, Charles C Thomas, Springfield, Ill., 1961, p. 160.
19. *Proc. S. P. R.*, 53, 1961, p. 245.
20. Crookall, R., *Intimations of Immortality*, James Clarke, 1965.

21. *Ibid.*, p. 23.
22. Richet, Dr. C., *Thirty Years of Psychical Research*, Collins, 1923.
23. Osis, Dr. K., Monograph No. 3, Parapsychology Foundation, In
   N.Y., U.S.A.
24. *Theta*, No. 15, 1966.
25. Smith, W. Whately, *A Theory of the Mechanism of Survival*, K
   gan Paul, 1920.
26. Leadbeater, C. W., *Man Visible and Invisible*, Theosophical Pu
   lishing House, 1907.
27. *J. A. S. P. R.*, 1932.
28. Garrett, Eileen J., *My Life as a Search for the Meaning of M
   diumship*, Rider, 1939.
29. Payne, Phoebe (and Dr. L. J. Bendit), *The Psychic Sense*, Fab
   & Faber, 1943.
30. Ref. No. 14, p. 17.
31. *Theta*, No. II, 1965.
32. Ref. No. 7, p. 139.
33. *Ibid.*, p. 165.
34. Whiteman, Prof. J. H. M., *The Mystical Life*, Faber & Faber, 196
   p. 58.
35. *Ibid.*, p. 60.
36. *Ibid.*, p. 70.
37. *Ibid.*, p. 74.
38. Cayce, Edgar, *What I Believe*, Association for Research, Virgin
   Beach, 1946, p. 21.
39. Hives, Frank, *Glimpses into Infinity*, John Lane, 1931.
40. Ref. No. 7, pp. 165, 184.
41. Ref. No. 34, p. 66.
42. *Ibid.*, p. 72.
43. Ref. No. 7, p. 52.
44. *Ibid.*, p. 43.
45. Ref. No. 3, p. 137.
46. *Journ. S. P. R.*, 43, 1966.
47. Ref. No. 4, p. 43.
48. *Ibid.*, p. 208.
49. Yogananda, Yogi, *Autobiography of a Yoga*.
50. *J. A. S. P. R.*, xxii, 1928, p. 47.
51. Ref. No. 7, pp. 42, 46–47.
52. *Light*, lv, 1935, p. 85.
53. Hankey, Muriel, *James McKenzie*, Aquarian Press, 1963.
54. Ref. No. 45, p. 41.

55. Ref. No. 7, p. 105.
56. Priestley, J. B., *What I Believe,* George Allen & Unwin, 1966, p. 166.
57. *J. A. S. P. R.,* xxxii, 1938, p. 374.
58. Ref. No. 7, p. 53.
59. *Ibid.,* p. 54.
60. *Ibid.,* p. 57.
61. *Ibid.,* p. 58.
62. *Ibid.,* p. 61.
63. Ref. No. 34, p. 66.
64. Ref. No. 7, pp. 17, 18, 27.
65. Anon., *I Awoke,* J. Stott, p. 34.
66. Wingfield, Kate, *More Guidance from Beyond,* Philip Allan, 1925, p. 28.
67. Ref. No. 7, p. 29.
68. *Ibid.,* p. 31.
69. *Light,* lv, 1935, p. 209.
70. Ref. No. 7, 9.
71. *Ibid.,* p. 11.
72. Ref. No. 34, p. 50.
73. Ref. No. 7, p. xxxviii.
74. *Ibid.,* pp. 6, 7, 15, 16, 70.
75. *Ibid.,* pp. 34–36.
76. *Ibid.,* p. 30.
77. *Proc. S. P. R.,* 1911.
78. *American Magazine,* March, 1929.
79. Crookall, R., *The Next World—and the Next,* Theosophical Publishing House, 1966, p. 96.
80. Paton, L. B., *Spiritism and the Cult of the Dead,* Hodder & Stoughton, 1921, p. 170.
81. *Ibid.,* p. 174.
82. *Ibid.,* p. 244.
83. Hughes, Thomas, *Tom Brown's Schooldays,* Longmans, 1857, Chap. VI.
84. Kernahan, Coulson, *A Dead Man's Diary,* Ward Lock, p. 57.
85. Leadbeater, C. W., *Text Book of Theosophy,* T. P. H. Adyar, India, 1912, p. 131.
86. Heindel, Max, *The Rosicrucian Cosmo-conception,* 3rd ed., Rosicrucian Fellowship, Calif., 1911, p. 97.
87. Richelieu, Peter, *From the Turret,* Graphic Stationers, Durban, 2nd ed., 1958, p. 38.

88. *Ibid.,* p. 94.

89. *Ibid.,* p. 152.

90. *Fate* Magazine, 1960.

91. *Psychical Research,* xii, 1928, p. 156.

92. Pole, W. T., *Private Dowding,* Watkins, 1919, p. 74.

93. *Ibid.,* p. 92.

94. *Ibid.,* p. 111.

95. Dowding, Lord, *Many Mansions,* Rider, p. 30.

96. Ref. No. 7, p. 74.

97. Davis, A. J., *Answers to Ever-recurring Questions,* 1868.

98. Ref. No. 92, p. 101.

99. Cummins, Geraldine, *The Road to Immortality,* Ivor Nicholson Watson, 1932.

100. Leonard, Gladys Osborn, *Brief Darkness,* Cassell, 1942.

101. Lethbridge, T. C., *Ghost and Ghoul,* Routledge, 1961, p. 145.

102. Ref. No. 45, p. 106.

103. Ref. No. 34, p. 77.

104. *Proc. S. P. R.,* 1915, p. 233.

105. *Ibid.,* p. 227.

106. *Ibid.,* p. 226.

107. *Ibid.,* p. 220.

108. Ref. No. 34, p. 73.

109. *Ibid.,* p. 141.

110. *Ibid.,* p. 77.

111. *Ibid.,* p. 75.

112. *Ibid.,* p. 73.

113. *Ibid.,* p. 75.

114. Salter, W. H., *Ghosts and Apparitions,* G. Bell, 1938, p. 78.

115. Gurney, E. (etc.), *Phantasms of the Living,* Routledge, 1886, 527.

116. Delanne, G., *Evidence for a Future Life,* Philip Welby, 19, p. 128.

117. Vivian, Margaret, *Love Conquers Death,* L. S. A., pp. 117, 153.

118. *In litt.*

119. *Borderland,* iii, 1896, p. 271.

120. Hill, J. Arthur, *Man Is a Spirit,* Cassell, 1918, p. 73.

121. *J. A. S. P. R.,* xiii, 1919, p. 274.

122. *Metaphysical Magazine,* Oct., 1896.

123. Leonard, Gladys Osborn, *My Life in Two Worlds,* Cassell, 19, p. 23.

124. Cornillier, P. E., *The Survival of the Soul,* Routledge, 1921, p.

125. Remilleo, *An Explanation of Psychic Phenomena,* Fowler, 1911, p. 48.
126. *Journ. S. P. R.,* v, p. 450.
127. Myers, F. W. H., *Human Personality and Its Survival of Bodily Death,* Longmans, 1907, p. 233.
128. *Proc. S. P. R.,* v, p. 450.
129. *J. A. S. P. R.,* 1921, p. 114.
130. Fitzsimons, F. W., *Opening the Psychic Door,* Hutchinson, 1931, p. 21.
131. Fodor, Nandor, *The Encyclopedia of Psychic Science,* Arthur's Press, 1933, p. 242.
132. Presidential Address to S. P. R., 1928.
133. Dahl, Judge, *We Are Here,* Rider, p. 18.
134. Longley, Mrs. M. E., *The Spirit World,* p. 2.
135. Tweedale, Rev. C. L., *Man's Survival of Death,* Grant Richards, 1909, p. 275.
136. Morse, J. J., *Practical Occultism,* Two Worlds Publishing Co., p. 8.
137. Vyvyan, J., *A Case against Jones,* James Clarke, 1966, p. 60.
138. *Proc. S. P. R.,* 33, p. 86.
139. *Light,* vol. ii.
140. Tappan, Cora L. V., *Discourses,* J. Burns, 1875, p. 94.
141. Ref. No. 13, pp. 123–25.
142. Osis, Dr. K., Parapsychology Monographs, No. 3, 1961.
143. Ref. No. 115, p. 215.
144. *Proc. S. P. R.,* 33, p. 378.
145. *Journ. S. P. R.,* Oct., 1932.
146. *Proc. S. P. R.,* vi, p. 17.
147. *Ibid.,* p. 95.
148. *Ibid.,* p. xxxvi, p. 517.
149. Ref. No. 127, p. 232.
150. Ref. No. 13, p. 12.
151. *Ibid.,* p. 86.
152. *Ibid.,* p. 95.
153. Tuttle, Hudson, *The Arcana of Spiritualism,* 1st ed., 1876; Two Worlds Pub. Co., 1900, p. 166.
154. Bardens, Dennis, *Ghosts and Hauntings,* Zeus Press, 1965, p. 89.
155. Roos, Anna Maria, *The Possibility of Miracles,* Rider.
156. Collinge, E. G., *Life's Hidden Secrets,* Rider, 1952.
157. Hitchcock, P. J., *Psychic Bedside Book,* 1952.
158. *Journ. S. P. R.,* xiii, 1918, p. 368.

159. *Psychic News,* May 21, 1966.

160. *Light,* lv, 1935, p. 209.

161. Oaten, E. W., *That Reminds Me,* Two Worlds Publishing C
1918.

162. *Psychic News,* March 26, 1966.

163. *Light,* lxxxvi, 1966, p. 165.

164. *In litt.*

165. *Psychic News,* April 28, 1956.

166. Curtiss, H. A., and F. H., *Realms of the Living Dead,* Calif., 19
p. 57.

167. *Quart. Trans. B. C. P. S.,* 1926, p. 383.

168. Hodson, Geoffrey, *Clairvoyant Research on the Life after Dea*
Theosophical Publishing House, 1938.

169. Moses, Rev. William Stainton, *Spirit Teaching,* L. S. A. Pub
cations.

170. Moore, Charles, *The Unseen World,* Moore's Publishing C
p. 11.

171. Davis, A. J., Ref. No. 97, p. 28.

172. ———, *The Physician,* 1850.

173. ———, *Harmonial Philosophy,* p. 133.

174. Tuttle, Hudson, *The Arcana of Spiritualism,* p. 189.

175. Roberts, Estelle, *Forty Years a Medium,* Rider.

176. Francis, J. R., *The Encyclopedia of Death,* 1895, p. 895.

177. Eliade, Prof. M., *Shamanism,* Routledge, 1964.

178. Schrenck-Notzing, Dr., *Phenomena of Materialisation,* Keg
Paul, 1928.

179. Rose, Dr. Ronald, *Living Magic,* Chatto & Windus, 1957.

180. Simpson, Colin, *Adam in Ochre,* Angus & Robertson, 1951, p. 2

181. *Proc. S. P. R.,* i, 1882, p. 135.

182. *J. A. S. P. R.,* v, 1911, p. 471.

183. Osborn, A. W., *The Meaning of Personal Existence,* Sidgwick
Jackson, 1966, p. 4.

184. Ref. No. 115, vol. ii, p. 211.

185. *Journ. S. P. R.,* viii, 1897–8, p. 321.

186. *Ibid.,* p. 330.

187. *Ibid.,* xxi, 1923–4, p. 291.

188. *J. A. S. P. R.,* xxi, 1927, p. 100.

189. Mueller, Dr. E., in F. C. Sculthorpe, *Excursions to the Spi*
World, Greater World Association, 1964.

190. Wood, Edith M., *Experiences of a Medium,* Arthur Stockwoo
p. 8.

191. *Ibid.,* p. 57.
192. Ref. No. 13, p. 21.
193. Ward, J. S. M., *Gone West,* Rider, 1917, p. 160.
194. Wood, Dr. F. H., *Through the Psychic Door,* Psychic Press, 1964.
195. A. L. E. H., *Fragments from My Messages,* Women's Printing Society, 1929.
196. Ref. No. 99, p. 87.
197. Anon., *Letters from Hell,* Macmillan, 1911, p. 3.
198. Fitzsimons, F. W., *Opening the Psychic Door,* Hutchinson, 1933, p. 35.
199. "Marmaduke," *The Progression of Marmaduke,* Stead's Publishing House, 1923, p. 47.
200. Stead, W. T., *After Death, ibid.,* 1897, p. 59.
201. Ref. No. 13, p. 12.
202. Wickland, Dr. Karl A., *Thirty Years among the Dead,* Psychic Press, p. 282.
203. Puri, Swami Omananda, *The Boy and the Brothers,* Gollancz, 1969, p. 106.
204. Ref. No. 133, p. 196.
205. Herbind, Charlotte G., *The Meeting of the Spheres,* Arthur L. Humphries, 1915, p. 73.
206. Ref. No. 13, p. 60.
207. Ref. No. 205, p. 224.
208. Ref. No. 197, p. 5.
209. Wallace, Mary Bruce, *The Coming Light,* Watkins, 1924, p. 94.
210. Ref. No. 124, pp. 8, 34.
211. Ref. No. 193, p. 21.
212. Bamber, Mrs. Kelway, *Claude's Book,* Psychic Book Club, 1918, p. 5.
213. Ref. No. 199, pp. 32, 347.
214. Ref. No. 13, p. 21.
215. Ref. No. 130, p. 82.
216. Robertson, F. T., *Celestial Voices,* H. H. Greaves.
217. Ref. No. 193, p. 28.
218. Thomas, Rev. C. Drayton, *From Life to Life,* Rider, p. 72.
219. Ref. No. 99, p. 76.
220. *Light,* xlvi, 1926, p. 88.
221. Fernie, Mrs. A. L., *Not Silent—If Dead,* Fernie.
222. Ref. No. 130, p. 82.
223. Farnese, A., *A Wanderer in Spirit Lands,* W. J. Sinkins, 1896, pp. 5, 9, 12, 16.

224. Brittain, Annie, *'Twixt Earth and Heaven,* Rider, 1935, p. 65.
225. Andre, G. G., *Morning Talks,* Watkins, 1924, p. 89.
226. Montgomery Smith, W. S., *Life and Work in the Spiritual Body,* Hillside Press, p. 59.
227. Trevor, G., *Death's Door Opens,* Rider, 1960, p. 30.
228. "Wilberforce," *Letters from the Other Side,* Watkins, 1919, p. 2.
229. Stead, W. T., *Blue Island,* 1922, p. 94.
230. Brandon, Wilfred, *Open the Door,* Alfred A. Knopf, 1935, p. xviii.
231. *Ibid.,* p. 97.
232. Denis, Leon, *Here and Hereafter,* Rider, 1910, p. 252.
233. Ref. No. 13, p. 10.
234. *Ibid.,* pp. 130, 131, diagrams pp. 205, 206, 209.
235. Ref. No. 79, pp. 54, 59, 62, 63, 92, 96, 100, 102, 111, 115, 116, 117, 118, 119.
236. *Ibid.,* pp. 3, 73, 110, 114.
237. Ref. No. 13, pp. 216, 228, diagram No. 5, p. 209.
238. Cummins, Geraldine, *Travellers in Eternity,* Psychic Press, 1948, p. 43.
239. *Ibid.,* p. 47.
240. A. L. E. H., *Fragments from My Messages,* 1929, p. 160.
241. Ref. No. 59, p. 221.
242. Ref. No. 117, pp. 137, 142.
243. Ref. No. 193, p. 47.
244. Ref. No. 13, p. 48.
245. *Ibid.,* pp. 137, 142.
246. Ref. No. 79, p. 47.
247. John iv, 14.
248. John vii, 38.
249. *J. A. S. P. R.,* x, 1918, p. 49.
250. Roos, Anna Maria, *op. cit.,* p. 93.
251. Ref. No. 7, p. 93.
252. *In litt.*
253. *London Forum,* March, 1935.
254. Gibier, Dr. P., *Analyses des Choses,* Paris.
255. *Proc. S. P. R.,* 1895, p. 45.
256. Cummins, Geraldine, *Swan on a Black Sea,* Routledge & Kegan Paul, 1965, pp. 34, 35.
257. *Proc. S. P. R.,* 43, 1935.

For permission to make extracts from copyright material, the author tenders grateful thanks to the publishers and authors mentioned below.

American Magazine: March, 1920

American S. P. R.: J. A. S. P. R., xxi, 1927, p. 101; xxii, 1928, p. 47

Aquarian Press: R. Crookall, *The Study and Practice of Astral Projection,* 1961; *More Astral Projections,* 1964; *The Techniques of Astral Projection,* 1964

Arthur L. Humphries: Charlotte G. Herbine, *The Meeting of the Spheres,* 1915, p. 224

Arthur Stockwell: Edith M. Wood, *Experiences of a Medium,* p. 55

Association for Research & Enlightenment (Virginia Beach, Va.): Edgar Cayce, *What I Believe,* 1946, p. 21

Baily Bros. & Swinfen: Dr. J. F. Laubscher, *Where Mystery Dwells,* 1963

Cassell & Co., Ltd.: Mrs. Gladys Osborn Leonard, *Brief Darkness,* 1942

Charles C Thomas (Springfield, Ill.): Prof. C. J. Ducasse, *A Critical Examination of the Belief in a Life after Death,* 1961, p. 160

Chatto & Windus: Aldous Huxley, *Literature and Science,* 1963, p. 7

Collins & Co., Ltd.: Dr. C. Richet, *Thirty Years of Psychical Research,* 1923

Faber & Faber, Ltd.: Lord Brain, *Science and Man,* 1966, p. 99; Prof. J. H. M. Whiteman, *The Mystical Life,* 1961, pp. 58, 73, 77

Graphic Stationers (Durban): Peter Richelieu, *From the Turret,* 2nd ed., 1958, pp. 38, 94

Greater World Association: F. C. Sculthorpe, *Excursions to the Spirit World,* 1962

Hodder & Stoughton: L. B. Paton, *Spiritism and the Cult of the Dead in Antiquity,* 1921, p. 170

Hutchinson: F. W. Fitzsimons, *Opening the Psychic Door,* 1933, p. 35

Ivor Nicholson & Watson: Geraldine Cummins, *The Road to Immortality*, 1932

James Clarke & Co., Ltd.: R. Crookall, *The Supreme Adventure*, 1961; *Intimations of Immortality*, 1965; J. Vyvyan, *A Case against Jones*, 1966, p. 60

John Lane: Frank Hives, *Glimpses into Infinity*, 1931

L. S. A. Publications: Rev. Wm. Stainton Moses, *Spirit Teachings*, 1935

Light: lv, 1935, p. 85; lxxxvi, 1966, p. 165

Longmans Green & Co., Ltd.: Thomas Hughes, *Tom Brown's Schooldays*, 1857, Pt. II, Chap. VI

Maby, J. Cecil: *Confessions of a Sensitive*, 1966, pp. 67, 68

Macmillan & Co., Ltd.: Anon., *Letters from Hell* (transl. Julie Sutter), 1911, p. 3

Parapsychology Foundation, Inc.: Dr. K. Osis, Parapsychology Monographs No. 3, 1961

Penguin Books: Dr. W. F. Jackson-Knight, Virgil's *Aeneid*, Bk. VI, p. 388

Philip Allan: Kate Wingfield, *More Guidance from Beyond*, 1925, p. 28

Psychic Book Club: Mrs. Kelway Bamber, *Claude's Book*, 1918, p. 5; P. J. Hitchcock, *Psychic Bedside Book*, 1952, p. 16

Psychic News: April 28, 1956; March 26, 1966; May 21, 1966

Rider & Co., Ltd.: S. J. Muldoon, *The Projection of the Astral Body*, 1929, pp. 68, 69, 75, 78, 144; Anna Maria Roos, *The Possibility of Miracles;* E. G. Collinge, *Life's Hidden Secrets*, 1958; J. S. M. Ward, *Gone West*, 1917, pp. 160, 358; Judge Dahl, *We Are Here*, 1931, p. 96; C. Drayton Thomas, *From Life to Life;* Mrs. Annie Brittain, *'Twixt Earth and Heaven*, 1935, p. 65

Rosicrucian Fellowship, Calif.: Max Heindel, *The Rosicrucian Cosmoconception*, 1911

Routledge & Kegan Paul: Prof. M. Eliade, *Shamanism*, 1961; Geraldine Cummins, *Swan on a Black Sea*, 1965

S. P. R.: *Proc.* i, p. 135; xxxiii, p. 86; 1911, p. 385; 1915, pp. 227, 233; *Journ.* iii, pp. 310, 321, 330; xxi, p. 291; xliii, 1966

Sidgwick & Jackson: A. W. Osborn, *The Meaning of Personal Existence*, 1966, p. 4

Theosophical Publishing House (Adyar): C. W. Leadbeater, *Text Book of Theosophy*, 1912, p. 131

——— (London): R. Crookall, *The Next World—and the Next*, 1966

Theta: ii, 1965; v, 1966

Two Worlds Publishing Co.: Hudson Tuttle, *The Arcana of Spiritualism* (1876), 1900, p. 166; E. W. Oaten, *That Reminds Me,* 1938

Watkins: W. T. Pole, *Private Dowding,* 1917, p. 101; G. G. Andrae, *Morning Talks,* 1926, p. 89; Anon., *Letters from the Other Side,* 1919, p. 2

Library of the Mystic Arts

A LIBRARY OF ANCIENT AND MODERN CLASSICS

ANIMAL GHOSTS by Raymond Bayless. With a Foreword by Robert Crookall, B.Sc. (Psychology), D.Sc., Ph.D. 5⅜ x 8″ $5.95   PSYCHICAL RESEARCH

In this significant volume, Raymond Bayless presents a methodical, scientific analysis of animal ghosts, and other paranormal and psychic phenomena found with certain animals.

With engaging skepticism, the author separates the "mediumistic chaff" from authentic paranormal experiences to present a remarkable series of verified case histories of animal ghosts and hauntings. In twenty-one fascinating chapters, he explores such topics as: Animal Hypnotism . . . Mysterious Abilities . . . Psychic Photography . . . Thinking and Communicating Animals . . . Animals and Mediums . . . Pseudo-Mediums and Mediumistic Chaff . . . Animals and Astral Projection . . . Materialization and Animals . . . Hauntings and Animals . . . Composite Phantoms . . . The Tweedale Haunting . . . A Mysterious Barking . . . Animal Ghost Stories . . . The Poltergeist . . . Witchcraft . . . Objectivity and Apparitions.

Bayless brings a delightful candor and humor to his investigations, as when he exposes a fraudulent medium, in Chapter VIII: "We were treated to endless messages from our departed relatives, . . . and this incredible communion with our dead became all the more awesome and majestic since our dear departed were all very much alive at the time."

The author demonstrates how psychic abilities and phenomena exhibited by human beings are also possessed by certain animals—and he points out the distinctive differences between the animal and human phenomena.

The distinguished scientist, Dr. Robert Crookall, lauds *Animal Ghosts* as a "really worthwhile book . . . the first comprehensive survey of the possibilities of animal extrasensory perception (ESP) and animal survival of death . . . a great service in giving us an authoritative review of this intriguing area."

Animal Ghosts is an exciting, provocative work—offering solace to animal lovers, food for thought to the general reader, and important new vistas to the serious student of the occult sciences and psychical research.

INTRODUCTION TO AFRICAN CIVILIZATION by John G. Jackson, introduction and additional bibliographical notes by John Henrik Clarke. 384 pp. bibliography, illustrations. 5⅜ x 8″ 75-92360 $10.00 ANTHROPOLOGY

With painstaking, objective, brilliant scholarship, John G. Jackson presents a portrait of a human heritage infinitely more rich and colorful and varied than is generally understood.

This book challenges all of the standard approaches to African history and will, no doubt, disturb the large number of overnight "authorities" on Africa who will discover that they do not really know the depth of African history and the role that the Africans have played in creating early human societies.

Star-gods, moon-gods, sun-gods, Osiris, the zodiac, the lost continent of Atlantis—the impact of the myths and legends of ancient man upon human history is analyzed here: *"Since the lore of astronomy and the calendar were the basis of much of the mythology, ritual, and religion of ancient Egypt, which in turn has profoundly affected all the great religious systems of later days,"* observes the author, *"we deem it proper to discuss . . . these ancient African cults and creeds, and their effect on other cultures."*

What must be one of the most tragic instances of near-genocide in all the ages is told in Jackson's devastating, poignant chapter, "The Destruction of African Culture": *"All told, the slave trade was responsible for the death of one hundred million Africans. The modern reader may find it hard to imagine the desolating impact of the slave trade on African society."*

John G. Jackson has examined rare, musty tomes and universal classics, obscure studies and celebrated works of ancient philosophers and modern scholars—men like Homer, Herodotus, Darwin, Haldane, Frobenius, Morgan, McCabe, Freud. He has drawn from the work of distinguished anthropologists, archaeologists, geologists, sociologists, evolutionists, psychologists, as well as conventional historians to present a vivid history of man's origin, his barbarisms, his glories in the vast continent of Africa.

THOMAS JEFFERSON VS. RELIGIOUS OPPRESSION by Frank Swancara 160 pp. appendices. 5⅜ x 8″ 70-105440 $5.95   POLITICS/RELIGION

This volume tells of the laws and decisions outside of Virginia before and after the American Revolution which imposed various civil disabilities for nonconforming opinion, *e.g.*, making the "Infidel" incompetent to testify in court, even against a murderer. It also contains a review of cases where criminal penalties, sometimes capital, were inflicted for avowal of disbelief in established doctrines or narratives of biblical miracles.

Here are the prelatic, priestly, and mobbish cruelties, impostures and coercions committed to aid orthodoxy and enable ecclesiastics to retain pelf and power.

Here too are observations on how it became possible in 1786 (and then only in Virginia) to obtain a Statute which would free from state **penalties or interference** every opinion or speech "in matters of religion."

OUT-OF-THE-BODY EXPERIENCES: A FOURTH ANALYSIS by Robert Crookall 208 pp. Appendices. 5½ x 8¼″ 79-97822 $4.95   PSYCHICAL RESEARCH

From the dawn of history to the present time, people have claimed to have left their bodies in various circumstances, to have retained consciousness, and subsequently to have reentered their bodies.

In *Out-of-the-Body Experiences: A Fourth Analysis,* a distinguished scientist applies the same rigorous procedure, on a psychological level, to such claims as he uses in a microscopic investigation of a petrified stem.

Robert Crookall, B.Sc., D.Sc., Ph.D., using scholarly, unsensational investigative techniques, has made detailed analyses of the testimonies of hundreds of individuals who have reported out-of-the-body experiences. *His investigations have revealed a remarkable pattern of events in out-of-the-body experiences.*

Crookall notes the extraordinary contrast in experiences of those who "died" forcibly or suddenly, as contrasted with those who "died" naturally or gradually. He compares the experiences of two different kinds of people: ordinary folk and those of a mediumistic bodily constitution. He describes in detail two distinct stages reported in some testimonies of out-of-the-body experiences.

Throughout this important volume appear significant insights and implications with regard to the concepts of Hades and Paradise, the question of life after death, the presence of "ghosts," and the meaning of the "silver cord" of the Scriptures.

MODERN AMERICAN SPIRITUALISM by Emma Hardinge. With an introduction by
E. J. Dingwall. 5½ x 8¼" $5.95   SPIRITUALISM

An extraordinary document by an incredible woman, *Modern American Spiritual-ism* is a twenty-year record of Spiritualism in mid-nineteenth-century America.

In this volume, first published in 1870, Emma Hardinge sketches the events preceding the birth of modern Spiritualism in the United States. She describes the varied work of the exponents of Mesmerism, electro-biology, and phreno-magnetism.

Chronicled here are the life and writings of Andrew Jackson Davis, "the Poughkeepsie Seer," whose works Emma Hardinge viewed as the beginnings of Spiritualism proper.

In her comprehensive record of what she calls "the communion between earth and the world of spirits," the author quotes generously from nineteenth-century documents and pamphlets, which today are virtually unobtainable.

She traces the curious phenomena known as the Hydesville rappings, which ushered in what believers call the first Spiritual Telegraph. She describes the course of events during the investigation of the Fox sisters, and charts the growth of Spiritualism in the city and state of New York, as well as New England and throughout the United States up to the end of the Civil War.

E. J. Dingwall, in his Introduction to this work, discusses the amazing events in Emma Hardinge's early life that inspired her lifelong Spiritualistic activities. In an age when "woman's place was in the home," this courageous woman journeyed over three continents, lecturing, writing, and serving as a medium.

Besides *Modern American Spiritualism,* Emma Hardinge wrote *The Electric Physician* and *Nineteenth Century Miracles;* translated and edited two books of mysterious authorship called *Art Magic* and *Ghost Land;* collaborated in compiling a hymnal, *English Lyceum Manual;* saw to publication of two volumes of her lectures; edited *The Christian Spiritualist;* and founded and edited three journals—*The Western Star, Two Worlds,* and *The Unseen Universe.* She was also an accomplished musician and composer, and became Directress of Music at Dodsworth's Hall in New York.

Recounted here are Emma Hardinge's astonishing experiences as a medium and magnetic subject, her supernatural experiences with table tipping and rapping, her participation in a Spiritual Telegraph, and her involvement in an extraordinary and disturbing courtship having occult ramifications.

Both *Modern American Spiritualism* and the story of its fabulous author provide the reader a fascinating panorama of a remarkable era in the history of American Spiritualism.